FOR BRITAIN
SEE WALES

A POSSIBLE FUTURE?

Joe England

T0348884

PARTHIAN

Parthian, Cardigan SA43 1ED
www.parthianbooks.com
© Joe England
ISBN 978-1-917140-28-7
Edited by Dai Smith
Typeset by Elaine Sharples
Printed by 4edge Limited, UK
Published with the financial support of the Books Council of Wales
British Library Cataloguing in Publication Data
A cataloguing record for this book is available from the British Library
Every attempt has been made to secure the permission of copyright
holders to reproduce archival and printed material
Printed on FSC accredited paper

CONTENTS

Preface

Author
Acknowledgements
Bibliography

PREFACE

This book is about the possible constitutional meltdown of the United Kingdom and its implications. For more than twenty years, Wales, Scotland and Northern Ireland have had devolved governments growing in confidence, taking policy decisions over increasing areas and being allowed to do so. Yet apparently this was hidden in plain sight until Brexit, and the different ways in which England, Scotland, Northern Ireland and Wales dealt with Covid-19, brought the devolution changes to public attention. The exit of the United Kingdom from the European Union raised three fundamental issues: who is responsible for rebuilding the devolved economies, who controls the funds that previously came from the EU to the countries of the United Kingdom, and how should those funds be spent? The devolved governments at Cardiff, Edinburgh and Belfast have one view. The current Conservative Government at Westminster has another. Its determination to centralise power undermines the powers and responsibilities of the devolved governments. An unresolved constitutional dilemma threatens.

The initial industrialisation and peopling of Wales collapsed in the first third of the twentieth century, was rebuilt on an entirely different basis after the Second World War only for that to fall apart in the 1970s and 1980s. The deindustrialisation of the UK, including

Wales, in the last third of the twentieth century, the consequent poverty in large parts of the UK, the exit from the European Union, the constitutional issues revealed, and the consequences of the Covid-19 pandemic are remarkable events compressed into a few short years. They deserve discussion.

The story comes in three parts. The first highlights the present and that Wales is the poorest nation in a United Kingdom where the former coalfields in England and Scotland – Kent, the east Midlands, Yorkshire, County Durham and Fife – have areas of deprivation. The once United Kingdom is now economically and politically divided. It was the stated desire of the Boris Johnson government to 'level up' this economic deficit by investing in the deprived areas. This remained an aim of the government led by Rishi Sunak. However, governments based in Westminster appear not to acknowledge the governance of Scotland by nationalists, the strength of Sinn Fein in Northern Ireland, and in Wales, the clear differences from England. These differences are expressed in sentiment and in practical action over the past two centuries, with, since 1997, a Welsh Labour government exercising devolved powers.

Part two briefly describes the historic flourishing and subsequent breakdown of the Welsh economy, the responses of the people, local councils and the Welsh Government to this economic decline, and the features inherited from those years of industrialisation.

Part three discusses the changes stimulated by the pandemic and the environmental crisis, the state of Wales today, what new Wales might arise from the old, and what kind of society it could be.

The pandemic highlighted the significance of the localities where we live and where everyday activities make our lives possible. For too long they were ignored until the pandemic opened our eyes and highlighted their inequalities and potentialities. There is a related issue. The, so far, United Kingdom seems committed to the seemingly never-ending pursuit of economic 'growth' in the face of clear evidence that in recent decades 'growth' has led to environmental degradation, comparative poverty for many, and threatens the survival of planet Earth as we know it. The deindustrialisation of areas of the UK that were growth centres in the nineteenth century, the attempt by Downing Street to assert central control, and the questions raised by a never-ending race for economic growth are intertwined themes. This is the story of how we reached these economic and constitutional crossroads and the choices to be made.

WALES AND WESTMINSTER

1

Britain and Wales

The legacy of unregulated wealth creation
is bitter indeed.
Tony Judt (*Ill Fares The Land*, 2011)

The United Kingdom, one of the richest countries in the world, is deeply divided. Oxfam, in January 2023, claimed that the richest 1 per cent were wealthier than 70 per cent of the population. More than two million people, and the numbers are growing, rely on food banks. The Joseph Rowntree Foundation reported in January 2024 that six million people in the UK were 'in very deep poverty', an increase of 1.5 million more than there were twenty years earlier. In the same month the Centre for Cities reported that relative child poverty had grown more between 2014 and 2021 in Swansea, Newport and Cardiff than in any other British city. The Senedd's Equality and Social Justice Committee reported that the Welsh Government's child strategy 'did not match the gravity of the situation facing children and young people in Wales today' and called for the appointment of a minister responsible for child poverty. More than one in four children in Wales live in poverty. Earnings of people in work show wide disparities. The highest earning neighbourhood in Wales in 2020 according to the Office for National Statistics was Heath, Cardiff, with an average household income of £58,300. The lowest earners were in Caerau at the top of the Llynfi valley with £29,100. These figures are not related to the size of families but are the earnings of people in work. In 1945, the British people – after two world wars separated by the Great Depression – decided it was time for a change. Let the government rather than the market provide a more caring future. Britain in the 1940s and 1950s was deeply in debt and recovering from the strains and damage of a world war. There followed full employment, a re-formed Welfare State, a National Health Service, compensation for industrial injuries, hundreds of thousands of homes to rent for those who could not afford to buy, implementation of the 1944 Education Act, free university education, a levelling up of incomes, and a general increase in prosperity.

Yet in early twenty-first-century Britain, much richer than it had been sixty years previously, the signs of poverty were everywhere. The Tressell Trust charity gave out 40,000 emergency food parcels in 2010, 1.9 million in 2019/20, 2.5 million in 2020/2021 and in the year ending March 2023 nearly three million parcels were handed out. In June 2023 the Trust reported that a fifth of the Welsh population faced hunger because they did not have enough money. Ministry of Justice data shows that 332 people managed by Welsh probation services were sleeping on the streets in 2023. A petition with 7,000 names submitted to the Senedd by the chairs of school governors in November 2023 raised grave concerns about the financial position facing schools in Wales. Home ownership is beyond the reach of many young adults; the 2021 Census revealed that almost five million adults in England and Wales were living with their parents. The Office for National Statistics described this as 'a continuous trend'. Yet the 2021 Census also revealed that 102,875 houses in Wales stood completely vacant, 7 per cent of all homes. A further 17,575 were second homes with no one living permanently in them. More than 10 per cent of homes in Ceredigion, Gwynedd, Anglesey, Denbighshire and Pembrokeshire were 'truly vacant'.

In ten years of Westminster-imposed 'austerity', schools, hospitals and local authorities had their budgets cut every year from 2010 to 2020. In Wales there was £800m less to spend on public services in 2019–2020 than in 2010–2011. Unemployment in Wales was the highest among the four UK nations. The budget announced by the Welsh Government in December 2022 for the next two years was a budget in 'hard times'. In October 2023 the Welsh Government, in an unprecedented decision, made changes to that budget, requiring all departments except health and climate change to make cuts amounting to around £600m to accommodate high inflation and necessary wage settlements. An extra £100m was taken from Welsh Government reserves to help pay for the changes. But in November 2023 health boards in Wales were required to reduce deficits by another 10 per cent, around £65m. The number of new apprentices has been downgraded from 125,000 to 110,000, despite protests by employers. The Finance Minister, Rebecca Evans, said, 'this is the toughest financial situation that Wales has faced since the start of devolution'. In England, Birmingham, Thurrock and Woking councils have all become bankrupt. The Local Government Association has warned that the risk of insolvency is now universal. Real wages are not due to return to pre-Covid levels until 2027, marking two decades of lost living standards.

Before the pandemic, Professor Philip Alston reported that child poverty in Britain was 'not just a disgrace but a social calamity'. He concluded: 'the bottom line is that much of the glue that has held British society together since the Second World War has been deliberately removed and replaced with a harsh and uncaring ethos' (Alston, 2018).

His was not a lone voice. The Nobel Prize winner Sir Angus Deaton was reported in *The Guardian* on 14 May 2019: 'There's a real question about whether democratic capitalism is working when it is only working for part of the population.' In February 2020 *Health Equity in England: The Marmot Review Ten Years On*, published by the Institute of Health Equity, reported that improvements in life expectancy had declined for the poorest 10 per cent of women; and men living in the most deprived 10 per cent of areas in England could expect to live eighteen fewer years than men living in the least deprived areas (Marmot). Research carried out by Loughborough University estimated that more than 90,000 people died in 2019 having experienced poverty in the last year of their lives. That is around one in seven of those who died. Since then relative poverty and in some cases actual poverty in the UK has increased. Stagnant productivity increased UK inflation by the greatest amount in thirty years and the National Institute of Economic Research predicted that 250,000 households would slide into destitution in 2023, making the total number in extreme poverty to be around one million.

Data gathered by YouGov in July 2022 for the Bevan Foundation found that the majority of people in Wales were cutting back on essential items. Between January and July 2022, 57 per cent cut back on heating, electricity, and/or water, 51 per cent cut back on clothing for adults, 45 per cent cut back on transport costs, and 39 per cent cut back on food for adults. Nearly four in ten Welsh households did not have enough money to buy anything beyond everyday essentials. As many as 180,000 households struggled to afford heating, food and toiletries. Six per cent of households had been told they would lose their home, that is more than 80,000 households. Nor are the problems confined to any one geographical area. Child poverty in Wales in 2023 was the highest in the UK, 27.9 per cent, with the highest levels in Blaenau Gwent, 30.3 per cent, and Ceredigion, 30 per cent, (Loughborough University). Even in Monmouthshire where child poverty is the lowest, more than one in five children (21.4 per cent) live in poverty. Eighty per cent of the children in poverty in Wales live in working households.

Before the Covid-19 pandemic, the Welsh Government asked the Fair Work Commission chaired by Professor Linda Dickens to report on the situation in Wales. This far-reaching report, *Fair Work Wales* (2019), comprehensively reviewed the Welsh labour market. It defined fair work as: 'where workers are fairly rewarded, heard and represented, secure and able to progress in a healthy, inclusive working environment where rights are respected.' It pointed out that productivity rates in Wales are low, workers in Wales are lower paid than in the UK as a whole, the prevalence of low pay is higher, jobs are often of low quality, and people in work suffer more from poverty in Wales than elsewhere in the UK. This poverty was projected to increase, as indeed it has. The report concluded: 'unfair work is a feature of the Welsh labour market and corrective action needs to be taken.' It recommended that public money should only go to organisations meeting or working towards the Fair Work Wales standard and that inward investors and large capital investments should be fair work organisations and 'Fair Work Wales' projects. These recommendations were accepted by the Welsh Government.

Much of the poverty in Wales, though by no means all, is in the South Wales Valleys, once a fount of technological invention and enormous riches for the owners of ironworks and coal mines, but now one of the poorest areas in Europe. Ill health, a legacy of the industry that once produced vibrant communities, means too many have slowly wasted away, suffering from pneumoconiosis, emphysema, bronchitis and lung cancer. In 2014 Sheffield Hallam University reported that, compared with other coalfields, the South Wales coalfield had the lowest proportion of adults of working age in employment, the highest incidence of those with bad or very bad general health, the highest proportion claiming Disability Living Allowance, the highest proportion of working-age people claiming out-of-work benefits, the highest rate of incapacity benefit claimants, and the highest level of multiple deprivation. In addition, there were just 41 jobs for every 100 residents of working age, hourly earnings were among the lowest in Britain, academic achievement was below the average in British coalfields, and 57 per cent of the employed labour force was in low-paid manual jobs compared with 48 per cent for Britain as a whole and 38 per cent for London (Foden, Fothergill, Gore). The Office for National Statistics published maps in November 2022 that showed the South Wales Valleys as the area with the most deprivation. Wales is just one part of the UK but it illustrates *in extremis* the failure of politicians and the economic system to guarantee even all those in work the security of a home and food on the table.

The greatest inequality in Europe is that between London and the South Wales Valleys (even though there is poverty and deprivation in London which the overall statistics disguise). Gross Domestic Product (GDP), the conventional way of measuring wealth, was in 2019 in Inner London more than six times (614 per cent) the European Union average. In the Valleys, GDP was 68 per cent of the EU average. That is, Gross Domestic Product in Inner London was nine times greater than it was in the South Wales Valleys.

Wales is not alone in its poverty. The Johnson government's White Paper 'Levelling Up the United Kingdom' published on 2 February 2022, which mainly dealt with England, asserted the need 'to end the geographical inequality which is such a strong feature of the UK'. All the former coalfields in Britain face similar problems to the South Wales Valleys. The deindustrialisation of Britain has spread across all regions, although despite having areas of deprivation, London and south-east England have increasingly prospered in the past forty years as the internal geography of social and economic inequality has become starkly evident.

That current conditions cannot continue was claimed as a major aim of the Johnson government. The Truss government that followed put its faith in enabling the rich to become richer in the belief that eventually extra wealth would trickle down to the rest of the population. Truss was swiftly succeeded as Prime Minister by Sunak. In seven weeks the United Kingdom had three Prime Ministers and Jeremy Hunt was the fourth Chancellor of the Exchequer in four months. Sunak became the fifth Prime Minister in six years.

In May 2023 a report by the cross-party Levelling Up, Housing and Communities Select Committee of the House of Commons asserted that the devolved nations were significantly worse off than when they were in the EU. It commented that there was 'an overwhelming sense' that the government's Department for Levelling Up was unwilling to adhere to devolved agreements. A Welsh Government spokesman claimed: 'Wales is £1.1bn worse off as a result of the UK Government's failure to meet its pledge to replace former EU funds in full.'

2

Can the Centre Hold?

'Take back control' may mean
'Let London take the wheel'.
David Melding,
former Welsh Assembly Member (2020)

In February 1945 when Roosevelt, Stalin and Churchill met at Yalta to discuss the post-war reorganisation of Germany and Europe the United Kingdom stood with the United States of America and the Soviet Union as a Great Power. In the years since then, the UK has lost its Empire, entered the European Union in search of a role, left it for the same reason and now the most centralised of all democratic states, the United Kingdom, is in danger of splitting apart. A fluctuating but persistent call from Scotland is for separation and independence. The Labour Government in Wales favours a federal United Kingdom believing that the UK is best seen as a voluntary association of nations. In Northern Ireland the majority of senators, represented by Sinn Fein, stand for a united Ireland. The elected mayors in England's great conurbations – Manchester, Liverpool, Bristol, Birmingham, Newcastle, Tees Valley, Sheffield, London – are using their powers and seeking more. The Labour-held 'Red Wall' constituencies

11

in the North of England felt neglected and voted Conservative in 2019 demanding better treatment. Late in the day Boris Johnson, then the prime minister, said devolution was 'a mistake'.

The View from Cardiff

The constitutional question had already been reviewed in a twenty-four-page Welsh Government document *Reforming Our Union* published in October 2019. This dealt with constitutional general principles, legislative and executive powers, finance, justice and the courts, and proposals for a constitutional convention to discuss the future of the Union. It claimed that the sovereignty of Parliament no longer provided a firm foundation for the constitution of the UK. The realities of devolution required further constitutional change and the Welsh Government was for an 'entrenched devolution settlement within a strong United Kingdom'. In twenty propositions, the document argued that the UK is best seen as a voluntary association of nations taking the form of a multinational state. It was a clear rejection of Welsh independence and an argument for a federal United Kingdom.

Westminster's Response

A year later the Johnson government passed the Internal Market Act and proceeded to assert the primacy of a United Kingdom governed from Westminster. Symbols were hastily brought into play. No Westminster government minister appears on television without a Union Jack in the background. Union Jacks fly on Westminster government buildings across the UK, emphasising that these buildings represent the UK Government. (Wales has never been represented on the Union Jack.) The railways will be renamed The Great British Railways, a brand that replaces Network Rail. The Great British Railways will contain a Region that covers Wales and Western England. The number working in Downing Street on how to preserve the United Kingdom has increased. All Whitehall departments were enjoined to recognise their UK-wide responsibilities. Civil servants are required to refer to the UK as one country rather than 'the four nations of the UK.' And, more than a symbol, Michael Gove was put in charge of a new Department for Levelling Up, Housing and Communities. In February 2022 he published a White Paper 'Levelling Up the United Kingdom' which argued the need for equalising the economies of those parts of the United Kingdom which have been 'left behind' by years of underinvestment and neglect. The White Paper does not acknowledge Wales as a nation or an economic entity but includes two economic regions encompassing parts of Wales and England – 'Menai, Mersey, Dee' and 'Western Gateway' which covers the area from Swansea to Bristol. After being sacked by Johnson in July 2022, Gove returned as Levelling Up Secretary in Sunak's October 2022 government. The White Paper acknowledged that significant economic change may take decades.

Behind these moves lay the government's main weapon, the Internal Market Act (2020) which reasserts the primacy of the Westminster Government over the devolved governments. It gives Westminster the power to bypass the devolved administrations and spend money on projects in Wales, Scotland and Northern Ireland as well as England that 'directly or indirectly benefit the United Kingdom.' The channel for this will be the UK Shared Prosperity Fund which is the British successor to the EU's Structural Fund. The Welsh Government has challenged the Internal Market Act on the grounds that it severely curtails the power of the Welsh Parliament, the Senedd. The Court of Appeal ruled that this can only be determined in connection with a specific law that the Welsh Government wished to make. In a YouGov poll in 2019, 63 per cent of Tory Party members were prepared to accept Scottish independence and 59 per cent a united Ireland in return for the UK leaving the European Union.

As a preliminary to the publication of Levelling Up, the United Kingdom local authorities and community groups were invited to bid for money for specific projects from a fund called the UK Community Renewal Fund. This was intended to show that not only was the UK Government in charge but that it was taking immediate action. Two of the boroughs in Wales, Caerphilly and Bridgend, despite both having areas of deprivation and formerly receiving European funding for that reason, were not chosen as recipients of this fund. A variety of local projects have been funded with more promised. Local councils have welcomed these Westminster-funded projects.

The Welsh Government was outraged that its devolved powers over economic development were being ignored and pointed out that this competitive process was totally different from the EU process of allocating funds based upon a mathematical formula of relative poverty: a region's Gross Value Added Per Head had to be less than 75 per cent of the EU average. The value of the funds coming to Wales under the EU's scheme was £375m per year. The money made available to Wales from the Community Renewal Fund was £46m per year. The Welsh Government has stated that Wales will be £1.1bn worse off over the period 2020–25 than if the UK had remained in the EU. In the new process the views of local MPs were taken into account raising fears of 'pork barrel politics'. The actions of the Conservative Government were described by Labour politicians in Cardiff as 'a power grab' undermining devolution, and a potential cause of confrontation between Westminster and the devolved governments. The complaints were ignored.

Westminster's Plan for Wales

The UK Government's *Plan for Wales*, published 20 May 2021, made clear the intention to support economic growth in Wales. The plan stated that there would be £40m to decarbonise South Wales industries including steel; at least one Free Port in Wales; £15.9m would be invested for electric heavy-goods vehicles to be pioneered at Cwmbran; almost £5m would be available for the Holyhead Hydrogen Hub project; there will be offshore wind projects in the Celtic Sea; 22,000 civil service jobs will be relocated from London and south-east England to Wales by 2030, mainly to Cardiff; £1bn will be spent to improve broadband services across Wales via the Shared Rural Network. Assurances were given that Wales would receive the same amount of funding as it would have received from the European Union. These assurances have not so far been met. In April 2023 Wales was allocated two designated Free Ports, one based on Anglesey and the other covering the ports of Milford Haven and Port Talbot in South Wales. The Free Ports will have simplified customs procedures, relief on customs duties and tax benefits. There will be eight Free Ports in England and two in Scotland. The Welsh Free Ports have the potential to create around 20,000 new jobs. The Welsh Government has insisted that the two Welsh Free Ports will promote fair work opportunities and prioritise environmental issues and the climate emergency.

The *Plan for Wales* was no more than an outline of intended actions. But the intention was clear. The Welsh Government would be a bystander (shades of 'Glamorgan County Council on stilts') as the Westminster Government, which has command of the funds, determines with local authorities where and how the money will be spent. Essentially the government based at Westminster has issued a challenge to the elected governments in Cardiff, Edinburgh and Belfast. Each devolved government believes it has greater understanding of the needs of its country than do those who work in Downing Street, and that it has a broader perspective on national needs than individual local authorities. In Wales the local authorities favour working with the Senedd but desire greater freedom to respond to local needs. Meanwhile Westminster remains pledged to 'level up' economic development throughout Britain.

In 2023, announcements in January and November allocated over £318m to projects in Wales from the UK Government's Levelling Up Fund. The projects included a new rail line from Cardiff Bay to Cardiff Central station, new walkways and cycle paths in the Vale of Neath, the Conwy Valley, Holyhead, and also to the National Slate Museum and the Neuadd Ogwen arts centre in Gwynedd, restoration of industrial heritage sites in the Lower Swansea Valley, a new engineering campus in Blaenau Gwent to accommodate 600 young people, the building of a leisure centre in Caerphilly, the development of cultural hubs in Torfaen, improving ways of travelling in Powys, transforming Barry Dock waterfront, renovating derelict buildings in Llanelli town centre, regenerating the Rhyl town centre, improving roads and the bridge in Newbridge, developing Port Talbot town centre, and increasing accessibility across Pembroke town. These proposed developments were gratefully received by local councils. The rail link from Cardiff Bay will receive equivalent funding from the Welsh Government and Cardiff City Council.

New Leaders

Mark Drakeford resigned as First Minister for Wales in March 2024 after serving five years in the post. His successor as First Minister is Vaughan Gething. In Wales and Scotland the nationalist goal of independence was set back by the resignation in 2023 of nationalist leaders Adam Price and Nicola Sturgeon. The resignation of

Adam Price followed a report on Plaid Cymru's failure 'to implement a zero-tolerance approach to sexual harassment'. This report, commissioned by the party's National Executive, made 82 recommendations to 'detoxify' the party's culture. These recommendations have been accepted by Rhun ap Iowerth the new leader of Plaid. In Scotland Sturgeon's successor is Humza Yousaf. Both new leaders have inherited difficult situations. In addition, the Court of Appeal has ruled that a referendum on the question of independence would be unlawful. Referenda on the subject of independence require the permission of Westminster.

Unknown Future

The next ten or more years will be dominated by the planet's environmental crisis. But in the UK there will be a lesser but serious question: will the UK constitution survive or will it fall apart? If the UK Government at Westminster did succeed in imposing its centralising will, that would be a remarkable achievement. The emergence of Sinn Fein – the party that exists to create a unified Ireland – as the largest single party in the Northern Ireland Assembly casts doubt upon Westminster's ambitions. The restoration of power-sharing in Northern Ireland after two years of paralysis, caused Sinn Fein to declare that a united Ireland was 'within touching distance.' In Wales the growth in self-awareness outlined in the next chapter underpins the antipathy towards Westminster dominance. Giving evidence to the Constitution Committee of the House of Lords in October 2021, the Director of Cardiff

University's Wales Governance Centre said: 'In all four territories (of the UK) the proportion of people who say that the Union should be dissolved or are ambivalent is over 50 per cent.' The flying of Union Jacks and the assertion of Westminster's central rule has provoked nationalist sentiment in Scotland and Wales as well as reinforcing in England the desire to assert the dominance of the UK. The domestic issue that will dominate British politics for the next ten or more years is whether the United Kingdom will be ruled from Westminster, or will the UK evolve into a form of federalism, a constitutional device common around the world; or will it break up into separate independent countries?

The jury is out. An increase in expressed Welshness is not necessarily an abandonment of Britishness. Westminster may eventually find it can only hold the Union together by giving away more power, resulting in a federal UK or even a confederal state in which the four countries in the current UK act as equals. That is not the view of the Conservative Party. It strongly believes in a United Kingdom ruled by the UK Parliament at Westminster. A relevant case was the discussion between Tata Steel and the Westminster Government over the future of the Port Talbot steelworks. The Welsh Government was neither involved in the discussions nor informed that the talks had reached a conclusion. Nor was the Welsh Government involved in the discussions that led to the second leg of HS2 linking Birmingham to Manchester being scrapped, nor those that determined the North Wales railway line would be electrified.

Labour leaders away from Westminster have asserted their distinctive views. In June 2023 the Alliance for Radical Democratic Change was launched. Headed by former Labour Prime Minister Gordon Brown, the Alliance included the Welsh and Scottish First Ministers Mark Drakeford and Anas Sarwar, and Greater Manchester Mayor Andy Burnham and West Yorkshire Mayor Tracy Brabin. It aims to end the centralisation of power in Whitehall and Westminster. Mark Drakeford spoke of the need for 'a new strengthened union which guarantees that no one will find themselves unable to eat or relying on a food bank; facing old age or illness at the margins of society... A union which offers strong devolution for all parts of the UK'.

The stage is set for a fundamental debate about the future of the UK where power holders outside Westminster will extol the federal structures of Germany, Canada and Australia. There will be discussion of what is essential for a UK government to control; about what could be, or should be, the devolved powers of a parliament only for England; what should be the constitution of a second elected chamber which would replace the House of Lords – smaller without inherited peers, with elected representatives of the English regions, Wales, Scotland and Northern Ireland. It will be argued that the British political system is antiquated, that people have legitimate concerns about the priorities for their own country, that the First Past the Post voting system should be abandoned in favour of a proportional alternative and possibly that the time has come for a written constitution. The current Conservative Government ignores such issues.

This is not unusual. The Westminster Government has long ignored aspects of Welsh culture, legal structures and its economy. It refuses to grant a bank holiday on 1 March to celebrate St David's Day, although there are public holidays on St Patrick's and St Andrew's days. Unlike Scotland and Northern Ireland, Wales will not receive funding from the HS2 rail project nor from the cross-Pennine Northern Powerhouse Rail system because they are labelled as England-Wales systems, although not one inch of those rail systems enters Wales. Rail infrastructure is devolved to Scotland and Northern Ireland but not to Wales. The loss to Wales is around £6bn. In addition, between 2024 and 2029 Wales will receive a funding cut of 0.1 per cent in cash from Network Rail. The electrification of the mainline rail system from London to Swansea was halted at Cardiff because of lack of funds. If the electrification had begun at Swansea and had halted outside London, it is certain that funds would have been found to complete the job. The Crown Estate, which acts as a trust for the king, has been transferred to Scotland and Northern Ireland, but not to Wales. The valuation of the Crown Estate in Wales in 2021 was £603m. A report by the National Infrastructure Commission for Wales has called for the devolution of the estate to a new body, the Crown Estate Cymru. This would have the sole duty of improving the well-being of the people of Wales. Air passenger duty is devolved to Scotland and Northern Ireland but not to Wales. Wales is the only country in the world with its own legislature that does not have a justice system of its own despite a proposal by the Commission on Justice in Wales, chaired by the former Lord Chief Justice of England and Wales, that this should happen. The idea was dismissed by the Westminster Government. All four Police and Crime Commissioners in Wales favour the devolution of policing. About 2 per cent of Wales' railways are electrified. In Scotland 25 per cent are electrified, in England 41 per cent are electrified. There was a time when these facts would have passed without comment. Not so today.

The constitutional future of the UK remains uncertain. A poll by YouGov in August 2023 found a majority in the UK in favour of another referendum on entry to the EU in the next ten years. Seventy per cent of those aged 18–24 would vote to rejoin. Such a referendum remains no more than a possibility. There is another possibility. Were Scotland to leave the United Kingdom, rejoining the EU, and if Ireland were to reunite, enabling Northern Ireland to once again be part of the European Union, what future for Wales? The current review of parliamentary constituency boundaries forecasts that the number of MPs at Westminster representing Welsh constituencies will in future be reduced from 40 to 32. The number representing English seats will increase by ten to 543. The approximately 180,000 members of the Conservative Party currently give the impression of being right-wing English nationalists, a dangerous portent for a United Kingdom. A United Kingdom that consisted of only England and Wales would mean the increasing absorption of Wales under Westminster rule. This, given the political majority in Wales and the development of separate institutions, would be unrealistic. Arguments for an independent Wales could gain increasing acceptance within Wales.

Faced with these uncertainties, the Labour Government in Wales has taken action. In an attempt to shape the future, it set up an Independent Constitutional Commission to consider and develop options for the constitutional future of the UK, to consider ways to strengthen Welsh democracy and deliver improvements for the people of Wales. The Commission was co-chaired by the former Archbishop of Canterbury, Rowan Williams, and Professor Laura McAllister of Cardiff University. The final report of the Commission was published in January 2024. It set out ten recommendations, three of which aim to strengthen the public fragility of Welsh democracy. These were:

1. The Welsh Government should draw on an expert advisory panel designed in partnership with the Senedd, local government and other partners. The priority for this panel would be civic education, subject to a regular review by the Senedd.
2. The Welsh Government should lead a project to draft a statement of constitutional and governance principles for Wales.
3. The review of the Senedd reforms should ensure a robust and evidence-based analysis of the changes including democratic accountability.

There were seven other recommendations:

1. The Welsh Government should propose to the governments of the UK, Scotland and Northern Ireland that the Westminster Parliament should legislate to secure a duty of co-operation and parity of esteem between the governments of the UK.

2. The Welsh Government should press the UK Government to legislate that the consent of the devolved institutions is required for any change to the devolved powers, except when required for reasons to be agreed between them, such as international obligations, defence, national security or macroeconomic policy.

3. The UK Government should remove constraints on Welsh Government budget management, except where there are macroeconomic implications.

4. The Welsh and UK Governments should agree mechanisms for a stronger voice for Wales on broadcasting policy, security and accountability.

5. The Welsh and UK Governments should establish an expert group to advise urgently on how intergovernmental engagement in relation to energy generation and distribution could be reformed to prepare for rapid technical innovation in energy generation and distribution, to ensure that Wales can maximise its contribution to net zero and to the local generation of renewable energy. This should include advising on the options for the devolution of the Crown Estate which should become the responsibility of the devolved government in Wales, as it is in Scotland.

6. The UK Government should agree to the legislative and executive devolution of responsibility for justice and policing to the Senedd and Welsh Government, on a timescale for achieving devolution of all parts of the justice system to be agreed by the two governments, starting with policing, probation and youth justice, with necessary funding secured, and provision for shared governance when needed for effective operations.

7. The UK Government should agree to the full devolution of responsibility for rail services and infrastructure to Wales, with fair funding and shared governance on cross-border services.

The Commission has not recommended any specific outcome – 'that is for the people of Wales to consider' – but it set out the strengths and weaknesses, risks and opportunities of each of the possible options – enhanced devolution, Wales within a federal UK, and an independent Wales. This report was seen by the Commission as just the beginning of a discussion within Wales and beyond, on the future of Wales. That remains to be seen; so far there has been little public response. The Welsh Government does not have the power to implement most of the recommendations. That power rests with Westminster.

Agreements with Plaid Cymru
In November 2021 the Welsh Government announced a 'Co-operation Agreement' with Plaid Cymru whereby

Welsh Labour and Plaid Cymru would work together for three years on a raft of wide-ranging issues, some extremely ambitious. This was a deliberate move against the centralising desires of Westminster and a strong statement of a Welsh government's desired ability to take action. In immediate political terms it gave both the Welsh Government and Plaid Cymru freedom to discuss issues of common concern. Agreement has been reached on a wide range of issues. The one with basic political repercussions is that the number of members of the Senedd will increase from 60 to 96 with equal numbers of male and female Senedd members. The cost of these new Senedd members will be considerably offset by the loss of four members of the European Parliament since January 2020 and that Wales will have eight fewer MPs after the next general election. The voting system advocated has, however, been heavily criticised (see Chapter 10).

New Planning Laws

The 2021 Census revealed the extent of second homes in Wales. The area of Abersoch and Aberdaron on the Llyn Peninsula of Gwynedd with 153 per 1,000 homes was second only in England and Wales to the south coast of Devon. Pembrokeshire and Ceredigion were also revealed to have increasing numbers of second homes. The response of the Welsh Government has been the introduction of new planning laws. Councils will be able to make amendments to the planning system. Homes will be classed as a primary home, a second home, or short-term holiday accommodation. Planning permission will be required to change use from one category to another. Changes to national planning policy will also give councils the ability to cap the number of second homes and holiday lets in a community, and there will be a statutory licensing scheme for all visitor accommodation. Gwynedd Council has already approved plans to manage the change of use of residential dwellings to second homes or holiday accommodation. The intention is to tackle the problem of local people being priced out of the housing market.

It has also been agreed with Plaid Cymru that primary schoolchildren receive free school meals from September 2024 with the Welsh Government allocating £260m to implement the programme over three years. £11m has been allocated to fund jobs for Welsh speakers in the four counties with the highest level of Welsh speakers – Ynys Môn, Gwynedd, Ceredigion and Carmarthenshire. The funding is part of the aim to achieve one million Welsh speakers by 2050. An Agriculture (Wales) Bill has been agreed. A Bill to set up a state-owned national energy body for Wales is expected to launch in 2024. Based on Anglesey, its aim will be to expand community-owned energy projects across Wales.

In June 2023 the Welsh Government announced eight new laws it would introduce. There will be a Senedd Reform Bill which will add 36 members to the Senedd; a Bus Bill intended to make travelling by bus easier for more people; a Disused Tips Safety Bill which will reform current laws affecting coal tip safety; a Welsh Language

Education Bill which will protect Welsh-speaking communities and increase the number of people who speak Welsh; a Local Government Finance Bill which will involve a progressive council tax revaluation of all 1.5 million properties in Wales; a Gender Quotas Bill which will introduce gender quotas for candidates for election to the Senedd; a Bill to eliminate private profit from the care of looked-after children; and an Electoral Bill which will involve the automatic registration of eligible voters and develop an electoral system for the twenty-first century. Devolution is not regarded as 'a mistake' in Wales.

3

The Long and Winding Road

Devolution is a process not an event.
**Ron Davies, former Secretary
of State for Wales (1999)**

The determination of the Welsh Government to tackle the economic and social problems faced by Wales springs from a gradual accumulation of powers and a confidence which has developed since first embracing the devolution of powers in 1998. It has been built upon the slow enhancement in recent times of a national identity, only comparatively recently finding an outlet in executive action. In March 1979 a referendum was held in Wales to determine whether there should be a Welsh Assembly. Of those who bothered to vote fewer than 12 per cent said 'Yes'. With so few voting in favour why was the referendum necessary? And why, eighteen years later was there a second referendum which recorded a tiny majority in favour of an Assembly? And how, since then, has the Welsh Assembly become the *Senedd* with increased powers and every appearance of permanence?

Wales was conquered militarily in the late thirteenth century, making Wales England's first colony as Martin Johnes has forensically discussed in his *Wales: England's*

Colony? (2019). From the mid-eighteenth century onwards, despite the umbrella of British identity, a sense of 'Welshness' can be traced through an awakened interest in the language and history, in the nineteenth century through cultural symbols, until in the twentieth century came administrative initiatives and eventually an Assembly, now the Senedd, legislating for Wales.

From the late 1730s thousands of illiterate Welsh children and adults were taught to read their own language by the circulating schools of Griffith Jones. They read the Bible of course but many read the history of Wales, *Hanes Cymru*, by Carnhuanawc (Thomas Price) published in 1742, as did the literate London Welsh, who in 1751 founded the Cymmrodorion Society and in 1770 the more populist and radical Gwyneddigion. Spurred on by the imaginative forger Iolo Morgannwg who 'discovered' medieval poems that he had written himself and the 'ancient' Gorsedd of the Bards that he had invented, members of the Gwyneddigion promoted the Welsh periodical press and encouraged eisteddfodau. Interest in the history, language and cultural difference of Wales continued with Lady Charlotte Guest's publication in English of her translation of *The Mabinogion* and Lady Llanover's invention of a 'traditional' Welsh costume. An attack on the Welsh language – which was allegedly cutting off Welsh people from 'the march of progress' – came in the Inquiry into the State of Education in Wales (1846) which united Wales in condemnation of this 'Treason of the Blue Books'.

30

Despite a large influx of impoverished English agricultural labourers who found more remunerative work in the Welsh coal mines, the number of Welsh speakers in the last third of the nineteenth century increased. The language was firmly lodged in mining communities through the internal migration of Welsh speakers from various parts of Wales (two-thirds of the population of Wales was in the coal-mining districts of Monmouthshire and Glamorgan in 1911), through local and national eisteddfodau, in '*Hen Wlad Fy Nhadau*', a song composed in 1856 that became accepted as a Welsh National Anthem, and in the religious services and social activities of the chapels. Nonconformity was itself a major characteristic defining Wales as different from England. So much so that the 1881 Sunday Closing (Wales) Act, a concession to the chapels, was the first piece of modern legislation to treat Wales differently from England.

Increasingly from 1868 the Liberal Party was the dominant political voice in Wales, this too marking a significant difference from England. The Cymru Fydd quasi-nationalist movement briefly flared and then died away after 1896 but further symbols of nationhood appeared. In 1889 the Welsh Intermediate Education Act created county secondary schools throughout the country. In the 1890s the Board of Education approved Welsh as an optional language to be taught in schools. In 1893 the University of Wales, encompassing the university colleges at Aberystwyth, Cardiff and Bangor, was empowered by Royal Charter to award degrees. The university college at Swansea was added in 1920. In

1907 a Welsh Department of the Board of Education was created and in that same year the National Library at Aberystwyth was established. In 1909 came the National Museum in Cardiff. The library and the museum, both in imposing buildings, marked the Liberal high-water mark of cultural nationalism in Wales. Just fifteen years later the Labour Party was electorally dominant. Its advocacy before 1920 of Home Rule was overtaken across the UK by a growing allegiance to pragmatic trades unionism and parliamentary politics as the path to progressive reform.

Concessions to Welsh Identity

After two World Wars and the Great Depression, the Labour Government of 1945–51 was entrusted with rebuilding Britain's economy and society. It set about this task enthusiastically. Recognition of a Welsh identity continued. In 1942 an Act of Parliament had legalised the right to speak Welsh in court. In 1944 the first Welsh Day in Parliament was held and from 1948 it became an annual event. By the late 1940s a majority of Welsh local authorities and Welsh Labour MPs favoured a Secretary of State who would speak for Wales. The idea was defeated in a Cabinet meeting. However, a further concession to Welsh feeling followed when in 1949 a Council for Wales was established with Huw T. Edwards, the Transport and General Workers' Union area secretary for North Wales, as chairman. Cultural awareness was morphing into administrative recognition.

In 1951, the newly elected Conservative Government appointed David Maxwell-Fyfe as Home Secretary with the additional title of Minister for Welsh Affairs. (Inevitably in Wales he was known as 'Dai Bananas'). In 1955 Cardiff officially became Wales' capital city. From 1950 to 1956 a Parliament for Wales campaign briefly flourished with Lady Megan Lloyd-George and Cledwyn Hughes among the activists. A petition in support gathered a remarkable 250,000 signatures but S. O. Davies' Parliamentary Bill received little support in the Commons. In 1959 the long-held desire among a majority of Welsh Labour MPs for a Secretary of State for Wales became Labour Party policy. Aneurin Bevan, in recognition of Wales' cultural differences, gave it his belated support. Labour lost the 1959 election but in 1960 the Conservative Government established the Welsh Grand Committee to scrutinise legislation affecting Wales. When Labour won in 1964, Jim Griffiths, MP for Llanelli and reforming Minister of National Insurance in the 1945 Labour Government, became the first Secretary of State for Wales.

The First Referendum

Despite this appointment, the Labour Government came under increasing pressure from the Welsh and Scottish nationalists. Plaid Genedlaethol Cymru, the Welsh Nationalist Party founded in 1925 (usually referred to as Plaid) had been of little parliamentary significance for over three decades. But the drowning of Tryweryn valley in Meirionydd to provide a reservoir for Liverpool promoted a wide feeling that the interests of Wales were ignored, a feeling enhanced in 1957 when the opposition of most Welsh MPs was overridden. Plaid had contested only four Parliamentary seats in 1951. In 1959 it contested twenty. Three by-elections in the 1960s shook the new Labour Government. Gwynfor Evans, the leader of Plaid, took Carmarthen from Labour in 1966 and Plaid candidates in Rhondda West in 1967 and Caerphilly in 1968, although losing achieved massive swings against the Labour Government, seen by many as not doing enough to replace the jobs lost in coal mining. The Scottish Nationalist Party won the formerly safe Labour seat of Hamilton. Under this pressure the Labour Government in 1967 brought in the Welsh Language Act which meant that Wales was no longer a part of the legal definition of England. In 1969 the Government set up a Royal Commission to look at the constitution.

Unexpectedly the Conservatives won the 1970 election and Gwynfor Evans lost the Carmarthen seat to Labour. But after the two general elections in 1974, which put Labour narrowly back in government, Plaid won seats at Meirionydd, Caernarfon and also at Carmarthen, taking Gwynfor Evans back to Westminster. The Scottish Nationalists won 11 seats and came second to Labour in 30 more. In 1976 Plaid took control of Merthyr Tydfil Borough Council. The Royal Commission on the Constitution, known as the Kilbrandon Commission, had reported in 1973 recommending an elected Assembly for Wales with limited legislative powers. Deciding that the Nationalists could no longer be ignored the UK Labour Government decided to hold referenda in Scotland and Wales in 1979 to decide whether there should be elected

Assemblies. In Scotland a majority of those voting were in favour of an Assembly but as fewer than 40 per cent of the electorate took part the Assembly was not formed. The 40 per cent hurdle had been imposed during the passage of the Bill by those opposed to devolution. In Wales there was a resounding vote against having a referendum: 20.3 per cent voted for a referendum and 79.7 per cent voted against.

Welshness Increases

Nonetheless, among Welsh politicians a sense of Wales as a separate polity from England had grown steadily, promoted by a series of devolved administrative measures. Creating the Office of the Secretary of State for Wales had been a crucial decision. Initially roads, housing and local government were to be administered by the Welsh Office. Twenty years later the Welsh Office employed over 2,000 civil servants who, operating within Britain's highly centralised form of government, had added industrial and economic matters as well as agriculture, schools and further and higher education to the Welsh Office brief.

Increasingly the national identity of Wales was recognised. In 1946 the Welsh National Opera Company was formed. In 1948 the Council of Wales and Monmouthshire was created to advise the Government on matters relating to Wales. In 1964 BBC Wales began broadcasting. The 1967 Welsh Language Act repealed the 1746 provision that the term 'England' should include Wales, and that year the Wales Committee of the Arts

Council of Great Britain was formed. The Sports Council for Wales was formed in 1971. The formation of the Wales TUC in 1974, the Land Authority for Wales in 1975, the Welsh Development Agency in 1976, the Development Board for Rural Wales in 1977 and in 1978 the CBI Wales, each marking a growing acceptance of the distinctiveness of Wales.

A deepening interest in the history of the common people of Wales resulted in the formation in 1971 of a Society for the Study of Welsh Labour History, an echo of its English and Scottish counterparts, and the regular publication of its journal *Llafur*. There had also been a growth in Welsh cultural institutions commanding international attention: in 1946 the Llangollen International Eisteddfod was founded as was the Welsh National Opera Company. The BBC's Cardiff Singer of the World project was launched in 1983, the Hay Literature Festival followed in 1988, the Arts Council of Wales was created by Royal Charter in 1994 and in 2006 the annual Swansea University Dylan Thomas Prize, the world's largest literary prize for writers under the age of 40, commenced – each project a sign of a growing Welsh determination to be seen and accepted on the world stage.

In 1979 Mrs Thatcher became prime minister and carried out a revolution which few had seen coming. In Wales, which she largely ignored, the powers of the Welsh Office increased with substantial devolution of administrative matters. A Select Committee on Welsh Affairs was set up to scrutinise the Welsh Office. In 1982

Channel 4 Wales (S4C) began broadcasting in Welsh after Gwynfor Evans threatened to starve himself to death if the government did not introduce it. The Welsh language was given equal status with English by the 1988 Education Act. The number of Welsh-language pop groups and Welsh-language comprehensive schools increased. Public spending per head in Wales grew substantially. The sense of 'Welshness' and estrangement from Westminster grew when the remaining coal-mining pits were closed. 'We voted Labour – we got Thatcher' was painted on a railway bridge in Caerphilly. The appointment of John Redwood as Secretary of State for Wales, a Member of Parliament for an English constituency, did nothing to defuse this feeling.

After Tony Blair won the election of May 1997, referenda on the establishment of Scottish and Welsh Assemblies were back on the agenda. The decision to hold them was driven by events in Scotland where Nationalist sentiment was strong. The referendum in Scotland was held in 1997 and resulted in 'Yes' majorities for a Scottish Assembly and for it to have tax-raising powers. The Scottish Nationalists who naturally supported the campaign were joined by the Labour and Liberal Parties. A similar coalition campaigned for an Assembly in Wales where public enthusiasm was suspicious of the influence of the Nationalists. Out of a total vote in Wales of 1,092,317 those who voted 'No' were 552,658 while those who voted 'Yes' numbered 559,419. The majority in favour of an Assembly was a mere 6,721.

The Government of Wales Act 1998 transferred the

powers of the Secretary of State to the Welsh Assembly and put upon the Assembly a duty to consult with business, the trade unions, local authorities and the voluntary sector. Gradually the Welsh Assembly became accepted. Under the 2006 Government of Wales Act, Assembly ministers were given executive powers, and certain law-making powers were to be devolved to the Assembly should a referendum be held on the topic. In November 2006 Rhodri Morgan, as First Minister in the Assembly, made public the pursuit of Welsh policies different from those applying to England.

A referendum in 2011 conferred upon the Welsh Assembly the right to make its own laws in areas devolved by Westminster. Unlike the 1997 referendum, it gave clear approval to the proposed legislative powers, with 63 per cent voting 'Yes', although those who voted were still only 35 per cent of those qualified to vote. The idea of a separate Welsh polity became more real, devolution becoming an accepted part of Welsh political life. This was reinforced by references to 'the Welsh Government' after the Wales Act 2014. The Welsh public accepted the Welsh ban on smoking in public places and a ban on single-use plastic carrier bags. The Wales Act 2017 declared the Assembly to be a permanent part of the UK's constitution, which could only be abolished by a referendum of the people of Wales. In 2018 the Assembly acquired yet wider devolved powers and in 2019 it decided to call itself the Senedd.

A Separate Polity

Gradually, through increasing cultural awareness, administrative actions and the steady accretion of more and more devolved powers, there had been a growing awareness of separate government bodies in Scotland, Northern Ireland and Wales. In Wales a depleted and largely absent aristocracy together with remorseless industrialisation ensured that for over 100 years ideas of social justice and aspirations for equality had found consistent expression: a belief that government action in certain areas could produce a better social order than the marketplace alone. The Covid-19 pandemic considerably increased public understanding of the separate powers of the Welsh Government. It brought home that the Parliament in London was not in total control of the UK. The Westminster Government made decisions for England while Wales, Scotland and Northern Ireland exercised their separate and independent powers, taking different decisions on lockdowns and their timings. Mark Drakeford, the First Minister in Wales, received daily attention in the press and on Welsh television stations, more than previous first ministers had been given in twenty years. He seemed clear and decisive in a way that Prime Minister Boris Johnson was often not. For those aged under 40 years, decision-making by the Welsh Government became part of the natural order. In the May 2021 Senedd election the 'Abolish the Assembly' party failed to win a seat. The long and winding road had apparently reached its conclusion. Devolution had indeed been 'a process and not an event'.

A Muddle

Yet what had been revealed was a constitutional muddle which the stresses of the pandemic and Brexit had brought into the open. Quietly growing for over twenty years, the separate parliaments for Scotland, Northern Ireland and Wales had each gone their own ways. The referenda concerning the governance of Northern Ireland (1973, 1998), Scotland (1979, 1997, 2014) and Wales (1979, 1997, 2011) had made clear the voluntary nature of participation in the United Kingdom. Differences of opinion within the UK were clearly revealed. Scotland and Northern Ireland voted to remain in the European Union; in England and Wales the majority voted to come out. Only in England in the 2019 General Election was a majority of Conservative MPs elected.

The future of the Welsh language, spoken by half a million Welsh people, remains uncertain. In 2017 the Welsh Government declared that the targeted number of Welsh-language speakers should reach a million by 2050. The 2021 Census reported that the number of Welsh speakers in Wales had declined from 562,000 in 2011 to 538,300 in 2021. One reason was a decline in the numbers speaking Welsh in traditional Welsh-speaking areas. Another reason was a decline in the number of those aged 5 to 15 speaking Welsh. Although the Welsh Government remains committed to increasing the number of Welsh speakers, an increase in the numbers of people coming to Wales from other countries may lead to a decline in the percentage of Welsh speakers even if the actual numbers of Welsh speakers were to increase. The

Office for National Statistics predicts that the population of Wales will rise by 5.8 per cent between 2021 and 2031. The projected population growth will not come from within Wales but will be driven by the migration of those seeking refuge from the most adverse effects of climate change.

Labour remains the dominant political party in Wales. In the May 2021 Senedd election, Labour received 443,047 votes, the Conservatives 289,202, and Plaid 225,376. Welsh Labour, favouring a federal UK, won 30 seats – one short of a majority – the Conservatives won 16, Plaid won 13 and the Liberal Democrats 1. A study by Cardiff University's Wales Governance Centre found in February 2022 that 71 per cent of the Welsh electorate as a whole rejected the suggestion that 'The UK Government is right to remove powers from the Senedd if it is necessary to maximise Brexit benefits.' These sentiments exist not only because of present aspirations and understandings but reflect social and cultural attitudes inherited from the past. Some history will explain.

WALES PAST AND PRESENT

4

Iron and Coal

Those were the days when coal was king and the
valleys were the throne.
James Griffiths
(*Pages From Memory*, 1969)

Wales in the nineteenth and early twentieth centuries was
largely defined to the outside world by its medieval
castles and its coal and steel industries which placed it
at the heart of the British economy. Millions of years
earlier the Valleys, carved in geological time by the rivers
that cut their way to the sea – Ebbw Fach and Ebbw Fawr,
Sirhowy, Rhymney, Taff, Cynon, Rhondda Fach and
Rhondda Fawr, Llynfi, Afan, Nedd, Tawe, Llwchwr and
Gwendraeth – had evolved into a poor pastoral economy;
the uplands providing grazing for sheep, goats and
ponies, the rivers rich with trout, the valley slopes
sparsely dotted with farmhouses and cottages. Romans,
Anglo-Saxons and Normans came and went but the coal,
shaped like an oval basin with the seams lying close to
the surface around its edges, deepest in the centre,
remained largely undisturbed. Sixty miles east to west
and twenty miles north to south, the coalfield, less than
a fifth of the total area of Wales, contained coals of a

range and quality rarely found in one coalfield. For millions of years this was unknown.

Yet in 1901 four-fifths of the people of Wales lived and worked in the South Wales Valleys, a society defined by coal mines, chapels, choirs, world champion boxers, village rugby teams, colliery explosions, strikes and radical politics. It was a civilisation built on the iron ore and coal that lay beneath the surface. From these overwhelmingly working-class villages and towns came the cannons for Nelson's navy, the iron rails for the first railways in the world, the coal that fuelled Britain's merchant navy and enabled the Royal Navy to rule the waves. The Valleys were at the heart of the British Empire. Roads, canals and railways sent to the coastal ports iron, steel, tinplate and coal produced by hundreds of thousands of workers, and in the process, Cardiff became a major port. Fortunes were made and much hardship endured but the people who came to the Valleys, immersed in their roller-coaster ride through two centuries of hardship, rising incomes and rapid descents into relative poverty, kept believing in a better future.

From the late eighteenth century people had migrated from the poverty-stricken agricultural counties – Carmarthenshire, Pembrokeshire, Breconshire, Radnorshire, Cardiganshire – and found their way to the burgeoning iron furnaces on the bleak northern edge of the coalfield – Ystalyfera, Ystradgynlais, Hirwaun, Pentrebach, Cyfarthfa, Penydarren, Dowlais, Rhymney, Tredegar, Ebbw Vale, Nantyglo, Clydach, Beaufort, Blaenavon. Towns that had not previously existed grew around these new ironworks, becoming the dominant form of urbanisation in South Wales. Skilled furnacemen came down the Severn from Shropshire and Staffordshire, famine in Ireland sent starving, desperate people across the water to Wales. By 1847 the Dowlais ironworks was the largest capitalist enterprise in the world with over 7,000 employees.

Industrialisation elsewhere in Wales had begun earlier. The copper ore that was mined on Cornwall's north coast took three tons of coal to produce a ton of copper. It made sense to transport the ore to nearby south-west Wales where there was coal. By 1750 the area between Neath and Llanelli was producing 50 per cent of the copper made in Britain. At its peak in the 1880s it produced 90 per cent of Britain's copper. Yet even at its height it is doubtful whether the industry employed more than 4,000 workers. Its swift decline as smelting works were developed in the overseas copper ore fields was offset by the rise of Swansea to Llanelli as the centre of tinplate production. By 1914, 90 per cent of British tinplate was produced there.

This was dwarfed by the iron industry sited along the heads of the Glamorgan and Monmouthshire valleys. There, the iron ore and the coal to smelt it were side by side. Iron was the material of a new age. Steam engines made of iron drove the new textile machinery made of iron. Iron bridges and iron ships replaced those made of wood. In 1804 the Cornishman Richard Trevithick at the Penydarren works had made a world-changing discovery when he put a steam boiler on wheels, enabling a load of ten tons and seventy people to travel from Dowlais to Abercynon. From the 1820s rails from South Wales snaked across Britain, Ireland, Europe, Cuba, and America where Cyfarthfa rails gleaming in the sunlight of the prairies opened the West. Rails from Dowlais crossed Russia awaiting, as the historian Gwyn Alf Williams dryly observed, Anna Karenina. In 1831 the population of Merthyr Tydfil was greater than the combined populations of Cardiff, Swansea and Newport. For eighty years the South Wales ironworks developed across the Heads of the Valleys. But in the 1860s in the face of competition and the cost of investing in the new steel technology, most of the Heads of the Valleys ironworks closed. The roller coaster dipped downhill.

A Feverish Exploitation

To make money the iron companies sold coal from their vast mineral resources. When Admiralty trials concluded that South Wales steam coal was the most suitable for the Royal Navy, ever-increasing opportunities for profits provoked a feverish exploitation of the seams of the central coalfield. Pits were sunk at Abertillery, Treharris, Merthyr Vale, Senghenydd, Maesteg, Caerau, Penallta, Oakdale, and above all, in the Rhondda valleys. In the south-west, production of anthracite coal more than doubled between 1840 and 1874 and then almost trebled between 1890 and 1913. Ammanford, Brynamman, Pontardawe, Ystalyfera flourished, as did Swansea, the port for the copper and tinplate industries and the anthracite coalfield.

The greatest development was in the Rhondda Fach and Rhondda Fawr. From 1855 until 1922 forty-four steam coal collieries were opened. By 1884 'the area was producing over one-fifth of all coal brought to the surface in the South Wales coalfield' (Chris Williams, *Democratic Rhondda*). In 1913 Rhondda miners cut by hand a record 9,610,705 tons. The population of the Rhondda area in 1851 had been less than a thousand. Fifty years later it was almost 114,000. In 1851 the population of Wales was 600,000. By 1911 it approached 2.5 million. In the 1870s production of coal of all types in Wales was 16 million tons. In 1913 it was 56.8 million. Of the 485 collieries in Wales in 1913, 323 were located in Glamorgan.

To feed the incessant demand for labour, thousands of Welsh-speaking Welshmen had migrated from the Welsh agricultural counties into South Wales. Later came the landless, poverty-stricken farm labourers in Herefordshire, Gloucestershire, Wiltshire, Somerset, Dorset and Devon.

In the last quarter of the nineteenth century the Valleys of South Wales supplied almost one-third of the entire world exports of coal. The rivers ran black with coal dust, the once green fields lay beneath the ever-growing coal tips. The terraced housing clinging to the valley slopes or jostling for space with road, river and railways in the valley bottoms often ran without pause from one mining community to another. The roads and railway lines ran north to south following the rivers, linking the Valleys with the ports at Newport, Cardiff, Barry, Port Talbot and Swansea. Based upon its earth-bound resources of iron ore and coal, the South Wales Valleys had become industrialised, its towns and villages owing their existence to iron and steelworks and coal mines. The sheer numbers employed in the mines and in the transport of coal affirmed mining's economic and social dominance. Welsh was the language in the home, the ironworks and the pit. Marriage between English-speaking immigrant males and Welsh-speaking local females played a part in eroding the dominance of the Welsh language, as did the policy of encouraging the use of English in schools. Even so, Welsh speakers in Glamorganshire outnumbered those in the rest of Wales. In the 1911 Census half the population in Merthyr Tydfil and the Rhondda were recorded as Welsh speakers. The roller coaster climbed to new heights.

A Moral Universe

Religious dissent in a variety of forms – Independents, Baptists, Presbyterians, Calvinistic Methodists, Wesleyan Methodists, Congregationalists, Unitarians, Quakers, even Mormons – was, with the language, a defining characteristic. It was a view of life and religion from outside the established order. Disputes over theological interpretations often resulted in the building of a separate chapel. The desire to worship in English rather than Welsh led to yet another chapel. To this day, the story of the shipwrecked Welshman who built two chapels on his desert island, 'one to go to' and the other '**not** to go to' can raise a smile. From Hirwaun to Blaenavon there were by the mid-nineteenth century some 300 places of worship providing accommodation for about three-quarters of the entire population. By 1914 the Rhondda Urban District had 151 Nonconformist chapels with the capacity to hold 85,105 people. With their Mothers' Unions, Young People's Fellowships, Sunday schools, Bands of Hope, *gymanfa ganu* (singing festivals), and competitive eisteddfodau, the chapels were centres of sociability, education, debate and self-expression. They were schools of self-government and significant supporters of the Liberal Party. They set the rules for the whole society, emphasising personal responsibility, self-discipline and respectability. They were a power well into the twentieth century. Cinemas and pubs remained closed on Sundays; the cinemas until the 1950s; pubs, officially, until 1961.

Despite the religious and social importance of the chapels, the bedrock of Valleys' culture was the character and conditions under which men and women laboured for at least twelve hours a day, six days a week. Women were employed in the ironworks at outdoor jobs requiring strength and endurance, carried out in all weathers. In the coal mines, women and children worked underground until the Coal Mines Regulation Act of 1842 barred children below the age of 10 and all females from working underground. The mining of coal became an exclusively male occupation.

Unpaid Labour

Women worked tirelessly at home. Hot water had to be prepared for the men returning from work who washed their bodies in tin baths in front of the fire. If the men were working different shifts, these tasks were repeated. The sick had to be nursed and, if the workhouse was to be avoided, elderly relatives looked after.

Gradually there came the trade union, the workmen's institute, and ultimately medical schemes, each a response to ever-present dangers and an expression of common values. In the iron and steelworks, scalds from hot metal and limbs mangled by machinery were common. The South Wales coalfield was the most dangerous in Britain. From the 1870s until the 1930s it accounted for 20 to 30 per cent of total British colliery deaths. (Ben Curtis, *Morgannwg*, 2014). Roof and stone falls, flooding, explosions, faulty winding gear, runaway coal trams, even disused mine shafts killed many hundreds in innumerable incidents. The total who died from colliery explosions and accidents runs into thousands. The following table does not include the injured and does not claim to be complete. Many more died from other relevant causes and lesser disasters.

Disasters that killed 30 or more men and boys 1860–1934

Date	Colliery	Location	Numbers Killed
1860	Black Vein	Risca	140
1862	Gethin	Merthyr Tydfil	47
1865	Gethin	Merthyr Tydfil	34
1865	Maerdy	Rhondda	81
1867	Ferndale	Rhondda	178
1869	Ferndale	Rhondda	53
1878	Abercarn		268
1879	Dinas	Rhondda	63
1880	New Risca		120
1887	Wattstown	Rhondda	38
1890	Abersychan		176
1892	Tondu		112
1892	Aberkenfig		112
1893	Great Western	Rhondda	63
1894	Albion	Cilfynydd	290
1896	Tylorstown	Rhondda	57
1901	Senghenydd		81
1905	Cambrian	Rhondda	31
1905	Wattstown	Rhondda	119
1913	Senghenydd		193
1934	Gresham	Wrexham	255

Deaths did not end when the coal came out of the ground, or miners retired. Thousands died from pneumoconiosis, their lungs choked with coal dust. David Bevan of Tredegar, a member of Carmel Baptist church, treasurer of his miners' lodge, died in 1925 in the arms of his son Aneurin. No compensation was paid. Pneumoconiosis was not scheduled as an industrial disease.

A Political Transformation

The initial establishment of working-class settlements close to the collieries developed through the nineteenth century, as the collieries multiplied, into the conscious creation of communities. First in trade union and then in political terms, collectivism became the institutional driver for fairer wages and work conditions. In 1898 after a five-month lock-out, the miners of South Wales finally gave up their separate district unions and joined together in one trade union, the South Wales Miners' Federation, 'the Fed'. By 1901 the membership of the Fed was 128,000, 80 per cent of the miners in South Wales (Francis and Smith). In 1900 Keir Hardie was the first professed socialist to be elected to Parliament when chosen by the electors of Merthyr Tydfil.

The storm centre of the new politics was the Rhondda valleys, marked by the Tonypandy riots (1910), the eleven-month Cambrian Combine strike (1910–1911), the Unofficial Reform Committee and the publication in 1912 of the syndicalist pamphlet *The Miners Next Step*. Along with increasingly influential Trades and Labour councils, the propaganda of the Independent Labour Party bore fruit. The 1914–18 war hastened change as resentment grew against profiteering. Every MP in Wales in 1906 was a Liberal. By 1922 the Labour Party (including in its membership the ILP and most trade unions) dominated local councils in South Wales and sent MPs to Westminster from the thirteen valley constituencies (Daryl Leeworthy).

Something else had happened. In the last third of the nineteenth century the basic requirements of a civilised society had been gradually put in place. A combination of Parliamentary Acts and local action had made available reservoirs, clean drinking water, water flushing lavatories, sewers, drains, gas lighting, elementary and secondary schools, playing fields, mutual aid health schemes, and workmen's institutes with libraries and reading rooms. Cholera was eliminated. Councils even began building houses to rent. By the early twentieth century record exports, full employment, an expanding population, successful choirs and brass bands, the security of the chapels, world champion boxers – Jimmy Wilde, Freddie Welsh – a rugby team that in 1905 defeated the otherwise invincible New Zealanders, industrial struggles and working-class victories, all had combined to produce a self-confident South Wales exemplified by Cardiff's imposing Cathays Park civic buildings, the restless buying and selling of shares in Cardiff's Coal Exchange, the constant movement of shipping in and out of the bustling ports, and the ubiquitous South Wales Miners' Federation (SWMF) whose activists within every village and town in the Valleys took the lead in community development. The only way was up.

The Great Depression

Then the roller coaster plunged to the bottom. One hundred and fifty years of economic and social development had visibly and painfully come to a bitter conclusion. Before 1914 only 3 per cent of the world's shipping used oil as a fuel. By 1939 over half of the world's mercantile fleets were oil-powered and the number of men working in South Wales pits had halved from 272,000 to 136,000. The 1929 Wall Street stock market crash set off a worldwide slump. Malnutrition rose as mothers gave what food was available to their children, pulmonary tuberculosis increased, there were soup kitchens, busy pawn shops, Hunger Marches, the Means Test, bitterness, disillusion and anger. The Depression was not only a huge economic blow; it was a psychological one too. On Sunday, 3 February 1935, around 300,000 people took to the streets in South Wales, one in seven of the population of Wales. They were protesting against the Unemployment Assistance Board (UAB) Act of 1934–5 which would impose means-tested cuts in benefits. In Merthyr Tydfil thousands of men and women stormed the office of the UAB and wrecked it, destroying records and ripping phones off the walls. On 5 February the Government announced a standstill order on the new regulations. The number registering at the four Rhondda labour exchanges – Treorchy, Tonypandy, Ferndale and Porth – on 25 May 1936 was 18,500. Forty-five per cent of them had been unemployed for over five years. That year there were 318 empty shops in Rhondda Urban District. In 1939 Wales had fewer insured workers in employment than in 1923, the only one of the Ministry of

56

Labour's Divisions in which that happened. Between 1921 and 1938, around 400,000 people left Wales to look for work; most were the young and fit, aged 15 to 39.

Two Nations

For there was another Britain. Richard Titmuss (*Poverty and Population*,1938) calculated that if deaths in 1936 in Wales and the counties of Durham, Northumberland, Cumberland, Westmoreland, Yorkshire, Cheshire and Lancashire had occurred at the same rate, age for age, as in the comfortable Home Counties, 53,951 actual lives would have been saved. There were flourishing factories in the Midlands: Morris Motors at Oxford, Austin at Longbridge, Vauxhall Motors at Luton, and at Coventry Armstrong-Siddeley, Rover, and Hillman cars. Coventry also had factories engaged in aircraft production and the manufacture of rayon. At Rugby the British-Thompson Houston electrical engineering factory recruited Welsh migrants.

In the industrial suburbs of London new factories lined the Great West Road and Western Avenue where radios, gramophones, electric irons and cookers, photographic film, and vacuum cleaners were manufactured, mainly for the middle and upper classes. Dagenham had its Ford motor car factory. This was a division in economic geography and society that, with moderation in the 1950s and 1960s, has increased ever since. In the depression 'Home Training Centres' were set up in Maesteg, Neath, Aberdare, Merthyr Tydfil, Ystrad Rhondda, Pontypridd, Ebbw Vale and Pontypool to train young women in domestic skills. Hundreds found work mainly in London and the south-east of England. The thousands of men left behind were, in the terminology of the time, 'idle'.

Sticking Plasters

Attempts at amelioration produced an impressive voluntary effort. Grants from the Miners' Welfare Fund set up in 1920, with equal representation from coal owners and the SWMF, constructed more than sixty miners' institutes and welfare halls. Grants enabled unemployed workers and volunteers to build over a hundred recreation grounds, playing fields, and open-air swimming pools. Allotment societies spread across the valleys. Educational Settlements sprang up in the Rhondda, Aberdare, Merthyr Tydfil, Pontypridd, Bargoed and other towns. The number of adult education classes increased. Coleg Harlech, a college for adults without qualifications but with aspirations, opened in 1927. But altogether these were no more than a sticking plaster on a broken limb. The need was for paid work.

European refugees from Nazism started the OP chocolate factory in Dowlais and Polikoffs garment factory in the Rhondda. A button factory started in Dowlais in 1938 and the Nuffield Trust financed the opening of a garment factory in Dowlais in 1939. The Government's attempts were feeble. The new steelworks at Ebbw Vale and the trading estate at Treforest provided work for just over 3,000 people. Despite large-scale emigration, the number unemployed in the South Wales Special Area in 1939 was 57,000.

5

Factory Wales

In 1964, when I started work, you could get one job in the morning, another one dinner time if you didn't like that one, another one shortly after dinner, and a fourth one before the day was over. It was booming.

Catrin Stevens
(Voices From The Factory Floor, 2017)

The 1939–45 war came to the rescue. The miners and steelworkers were finally needed. Thousands of otherwise unemployed men joined the armed forces. So did women. In Wales the war began a social revolution. When Woolwich Arsenal was dispersed to the provinces, thousands of women worked in the munitions factories at Treforest, Glascoed, Hirwaun, Bridgend and Pembrey. In 1921 there had been just over four occupied males to every one occupied female in Wales. Fifty years later, there were just over two men for each woman in the Welsh occupied population (Williams and Boyns). More, the entire increase in the Welsh labour force of some 80,000 during 1971–81 was accounted for by women, as the male labour force fell by 5,000 and the female labour force increased by 86,000 (George and Mainwaring).

The New Factories

The Depression years were seen as the result of 'having too many eggs in one basket'. Wales had to import capital, technological know-how and entrepreneurial skills just as it had in its original 'take-off' to industrial growth. Factories were built at government expense and firms obliged to move into them. From 1945 to 1950 nineteen million square feet of factory space was approved in South Wales. The ordnance factories at Hirwaun and Bridgend became industrial estates. The Treforest estate already existed. A new estate was created at Fforestfach, Swansea. By vigorous use of the Distribution of Industry Act (1945) and the Town and Country Planning Act (1947) major employers came to the Valleys, steadily increasing the numbers employed. Among the new firms were Murphy and Sobell, at Hirwaun; Hoover Washing Machines, Teddington Aircraft Controls, Thorn Electrical Industries, Lines Bros/Tri-ang Toys, all at Merthyr Tydfil; Dunlop Semtex, Brynmawr; Anglo-Celtic Watch factory (known to the locals as 'the tick-tock'), Ystradgynlais; British Nylon Spinners, Pontypool; AB Electronics, Abercynon. The factories producing electrical switchgear at Blackwood and cables at Aberdare expanded.

By the early 1950s unemployment in Wales was consistently below 3 per cent. The Macmillan and Wilson governments brought the Ford Motor Company to Swansea, Revlon cosmetics to Maesteg, Johnson and Johnson to Pontllanfraith, Borg Warner to Kenfig Hill, Austin-Crompton Parkinson to Tredegar, 3Ms to

Gorseinon, and Girlings to Cwmbran. Factories not actually within the Valleys were encouraged to be 'within reasonable travelling distance'. By 1970 over 200,000 workers were employed in manufacturing in South Wales, more than coal and steel combined. In North Wales, Hotpoint washing machine factory opened in Llandudno, Ferodo and Bernard Wardle factories went to Caernarfon. The Rio Tinto Company established an aluminium works on Anglesey in 1970. The nuclear power station at Trawsfynydd became operational in 1965 and Wylfa Head nuclear power station began operations on Anglesey in 1971.

After the Depression years it was a time of extraordinary economic growth. The Severn Bridge, the M4, the three-lane A465 leading to the M50, the massive steelworks at Port Talbot ('Treasure Island') and Llanwern ('Eldorado') drew – from a wide area including the Valleys – process workers, craftsmen, draughtsmen, metallurgists, office workers, accountants, managers and administrators. The Trustee Savings Bank in Port Talbot was known as the Rowing Club. 'The Company puts our money in there on a Thursday and by lunchtime we've take it out. In, out. In, out.' The huge working-men's clubs at Port Talbot were reputed to have bar takings of well over £100,000 a year. There were modern tinplate works at Trostre and Felindre. By 1963 Wales was producing all of the UK's tinplate and almost all of the UK output of sheet metal, the basic material for the vehicle and consumer durable industries. In 1965 the major steelworks in Wales employed 70,650 workers and were the drivers of a new Welsh economy. There were new pits at Abernant and Cynheidre, factories in or close to the Valleys, and on the coast, chemical works. Milford Haven became the largest oil port in Britain. The Royal Mint moved from London to Llantrisant. To be 'left behind' while the college boys and girls went out into the wide world was not so bad. Apprenticeships with the steel companies, with the National Coal Board and with the modern factories led to good jobs with decent pay, better than earned by most graduates.

Service employments grew. The Driver and Vehicle Licensing Centre (DVLC) and the Land Registry went to Swansea, a new Passport Office went to Newport, Companies House to Cardiff. There were large new hospitals in the north and the south. By 1974 the majority of Welsh workers were working in education, health, public administration, transport and communications, retail, hotels and catering. But a price had to be paid.

Never-ending Change

The price was the extinction of the former sheet and tinplate hand-mills and the open-hearth steelworks that had supplied them. In 1950 there were 36 old-style tinplate mills. Eleven years later there were none. In 1946 there were 20 small steelworks in existence; by the early 1970s all had disappeared. The occupational and cultural bases of Llanelli, Pontardulais, Gorseinon, Gowerton, Pontardawe, Morriston, Briton Ferry, Pontypool, and Risca changed drastically. The new collieries meant the closure of uneconomic pits. By 1973 there were just 53 pits in South Wales employing 35,000. Former miners became production workers in the new factories. Similar colliery closures took place in North Wales. There also the slate industry was in terminal decline. Nonetheless, 9.1 per cent of the Welsh male labour force was employed in mining in 1976 and 14.5 per cent in metal manufacture, more than any other UK region (Phil Cooke).

South Wales appeared to be blooming, but it was a false dawn. Technological change and increasing international competition, particularly from Japan, brought huge changes to the steel industry. The East Moors Works at Cardiff closed in 1978, causing almost 4,000 to lose their jobs. At Shotton in North Wales steel-making ended in 1980 and 6,400 jobs were lost. Another 5,000 became redundant at Ebbw Vale as iron and steel-making (not tinplate production) were scaled down before the plant closed completely in 2002. At Felindre, tinplate production ceased in 1968 when the works closed. Steel-making at Llanwern ended in 2001. Non-recruitment, productivity deals and early retirements accounted for over 20,000 lost steel jobs by the early 1980s, even before the final closures. The original *raison d'etre* of coalfield towns disappeared as pits continued to close. Men no longer walked together to work in the local pit. The new factories and the growth of service employments brought a diversity of occupations and work sites. Thousands of women were in wage employment, a complete break from male domination of two centuries of Welsh industrialisation. It also meant a sharp decline in earnings compared to those that men had earned in the steel and coal industries. Much of the female employment was in low-level assembly work and there was little requirement in these 'branch plants' for high technical, research or managerial skills. Largely controlled by companies outside Wales, the employment they brought was increasingly dependent upon external control. Nonetheless, for some twenty years the new factories with their children's and Christmas parties, social and sports clubs and greater mingling of the sexes at work seemed to offer a new social glue. Then those factories closed too.

So did the miners' institutes, their libraries broken up and bought by second-hand dealers. (Some libraries were saved and stored at the Miners' Library at Swansea University.) Churches and chapels found their congregations dwindling as people encountered new experiences outside their coalfield town. The congregations became increasingly elderly, emphasising the widening gap between generations. In 1945 there had been thirteen MPs in Wales sponsored by the National Union of Mineworkers (NUM). In 1974 none of the Welsh MPs were sponsored by the NUM. From the 1940s to the 1970s great economic and social changes had taken place, but in towns and villages the lines upon lines of terraced houses remained. In 1974 the growing threat to the existence of Valleys' communities led to a series of conferences to examine the way forward. A record of these conferences appears in a volume edited by Paul Ballard and Erastus Jones (*The Valleys Call*). The spirit and strength of community was not extinct, but it was about to be challenged further.

6

'No Such Thing As Society'
Margaret Thatcher

In 1979 Margaret Thatcher as prime minister carried out a revolution which few had seen coming. She espoused an economic orthodoxy labelled 'neoliberalism'. Its essence was that competitive markets were superior to public bodies and individuals were free to sink or swim in these competitive environments.

Nationalised industries were privatised, valuable companies were sold to foreign investors. Unemployment in the UK rose to three million and from 1982 to 1987 stayed there, the largest total since the 1930s. After falling back, it rose again to over two million in early 1991 and reached almost three million again by early 1993. Norman Lamont, the Chancellor of the Exchequer, explained: 'Rising unemployment and the recession have been the price that we've had to pay to get inflation down. That is a price well worth paying.'

A UK thirteen-week steel industry strike from January to April 1980 over pay and jobs ended in pay increases but within days there were negotiations over redundancy packages and job losses. Almost 7,000 steelworks jobs disappeared at Port Talbot and 4,500 at Llanwern. The year-long national coal strike against UK pit closures began in March 1984 and ended in March 1985. A major aspect of the strike in South Wales was the women's support groups, conscious of the threat to communities if the pits closed. The spirit of community was still very much alive but within ten months of the end of the strike, nine collieries in South Wales closed. Others followed and by 1992 all nationalised South Wales' pits had closed. Tower colliery at Hirwaun was saved from closure by a workers' buy-out but eventually closed in 2008. A number of privately owned levels and pits remained but in 2023 the largest opencast site in Europe at Ffos-y-Fran, Merthyr Tydfil, was refused permission to continue. Thirty years earlier, as a major industry and way of life, underground mining of coal in South Wales had moved from economic dominance to practical extinction. The change had been summarised and forecast by Max Boyce: 'The pit-head baths is a supermarket now.'

A Global System

Privatisation increased. British Telecom was sold to investors in 1984, British Gas in 1986. The asset-rich professional classes in London and the Home Counties became even richer when the 'Big Bang' of 1986 made the financial sector of the City of London a law unto itself. The banks were deregulated, the financial sector trebled in size, a global financial system emerged devoted to making money out of the manipulation of money rather than providing goods and services. The production of goods was increasingly organised around global supply chains with companies looking around the world for the cheapest labour. 'Globalisation', a worldwide phenomenon as the name implies, took hold in the Regan-Thatcher era and remained a feature of the succeeding Major, Blair, and Brown British governments. Citizens increasingly became customers. More than two million council houses were sold with local councils banned from building new ones. Today, more than 40 per cent of former council homes are owned by private landlords who rent them out at three to four times the cost of social housing rents.

The 'wets' within Thatcher's Cabinet – Heseltine, Walker, Hunt – and those with a particular attachment to Wales – Nicholas Edwards and Wyn Roberts – did much to modernise the Welsh economy. A second Severn Bridge was built, the A470 from Cardiff to Merthyr Tydfil became a dual carriageway, the M4 was extended, the A55, the North Wales superhighway eventually linking Holyhead to Chester, continued to be updated. At Broughton, the Airbus factory grew to employ more than 6,000 with supply chains employing a further 2,000. The Cardiff Bay Barrage, strongly promoted by Nicholas Edwards, was completed in 1999. Taking advantage of unemployment and low wages in Wales, the Wales TUC, the Welsh Development Agency and Secretaries of State for Wales collaborated to bring more inward investment to Wales than to any other part of the UK. In 1979 there were 177 foreign firms in Wales employing over 55,000 people. By 1993 the number of 'overseas-owned production units' in Wales was 348 employing 68,000 people (England, 2004).

Few of these 'branch factories' providing semi-skilled assembly work came to the Valleys. Where once the coastal ports – Newport, Cardiff, Swansea – had depended for their growth upon the products of the industrial valleys, increasingly from the 1970s onwards the valley towns were dependent upon the manufacturing and service jobs provided on the coast and near the M4. Early retirements and 'going on the sick' became alternatives to unemployment, a tactic encouraged by the Conservative Government to make the level of unemployment less visible. Despite the initial increase in 'branch factories' and consequent employment, 'globalisation', the main thrust of the Thatcher government, steadily reversed this trend. Between 1975 and 2001 Wales lost 90 per cent of its jobs in energy and 40 per cent of jobs in manufacturing. Relatively well-paid, skilled full-time jobs in the basic industries steadily disappeared, as did apprenticeships. In just forty years Factory Wales had flourished and declined. The Welsh roller coaster was sliding ever faster downhill.

7

Up and Down

That's the way the money goes.
Pop goes the weasel.
W.R. Mandale (1853)

The election of Tony Blair's Labour Government in 1997
made a difference. Employment in services grew, the
homeless largely left the streets, greater attention was
paid to defeating crime, and the National Minimum Wage
Act 1998, effective from April 1999, was a welcome,
albeit an inadequate, response to the disappearance of
industrial jobs and the decline of trade union influence.
A narrowly won referendum on Welsh devolution meant
that in 1998 the Welsh Assembly Government was
created. So too was a Scottish Parliament. In Northern
Ireland the Blair government successfully defused armed
struggles by the IRA. In 2007 Blair was succeeded as
Prime Minister by Gordon Brown.

But factories continued to depart to East Asia and
Eastern Europe where labour was cheap and legislative
protection for workers poor. Apprenticeships became
scarce. The designation of West Wales and the Valleys by
the European Union as an 'Objective One' area in 2000
meant that it qualified for financial aid to bring it closer

to EU social and economic standards. Over £1.5bn from the EU was invested in infrastructure projects including training schemes for the unemployed.

Austerity and Brexit

In 2008–2009 came the banking crash. The coalition government of Tories and Liberal Democrats elected in 2010 to succeed Gordon Brown's administration imposed austerity cuts to council budgets, the NHS, police and other public services and implemented the welfare reforms known as Universal Credit. The gulf between the old industrial areas and the wealth and political power in the south-east of England deepened. In 2020, before the Covid-19 pandemic, over 76,000 workers in Wales did not have job security. They were non-permanent workers, part of the 'gig' economy on zero-hours contracts, without a guaranteed minimum number of hours of work. Their number had grown by almost 50 per cent since 2014. In addition, the number of self-employed people grew until in 2021 they exceeded the entire number of manufacturing jobs in Wales. Four of the poorest local authorities in Wales were the former mining areas of Blaenau Gwent, Merthyr Tydfil, Rhondda Cynon Taf (RCT) and Caerphilly.

'Taking Back Control'

In 2016 the referendum on whether to remain a member of the European Union was held. Against a background of inadequate and insufficient housing, poor transport, an underfunded NHS, schools and colleges desperate for cash, stagnant real wages, serious child poverty, people sleeping on the streets, boarded-up shops, food banks – the modern soup kitchens but this time a resort for 'the working poor' – mental and physical poor health, underpaid and insecure employment, low productivity and a de-skilled labour force it is not surprising that the slogan 'Take Back Control' resonated so strongly in the Valleys. Messages on social media that talked of 'floods of foreigners' found fertile ground. It was an opportunity to vent the frustration felt by men in the old industrial areas of Britain who had been thrown out of work with no alternative.

The United Kingdom voted to leave the European Union. In the Welsh Valleys the 'Leave' vote was resounding: 62 per cent in Blaenau Gwent, 59.8 per cent in Torfaen and in Caerphilly, in Neath Port Talbot 56.8, Merthyr Tydfil 56.4 and in Rhondda Cynon Taf 53.7. It was a cry of anger by those 'left behind' without 'decent jobs', neglected by successive British governments which had concentrated on making the City of London and the south-east of England centres of wealth. It was a world that post-war Prime Ministers Clement Attlee and Harold Macmillan had rejected more than sixty years previously. In the 2019 General Election every Valley constituency, unlike the English former coalfields, returned Labour MPs. But in every one of the central Valleys' constituencies there was a swing in voting away from Labour. Loyalty won but Boris Johnson's arguments for Brexit appealed to many. When there is no sign of improvement, why not vote for something different?

Just six years later, without any improvement in local economies, a poll by Focaldata registered that in all forty Welsh constituencies and throughout Britain as a whole, a majority believed that leaving the European Union had been a mistake. In 2016 in Blaenau Gwent 62 per cent voted to leave. In 2022, 48 per cent thought that leaving the EU was a bad idea, with 33 per cent thinking it was a good idea and the rest saying they did not know. In May 2023 a poll of British voters by Focaldata found that three times as many adults (63 per cent) believed that Brexit had created more problems than it had solved, compared with 21 per cent who believed it had solved more than it had created. Of those polled 53 per cent wanted a closer relationship with the EU.

The Inheritance

Leaving the European Union had been presented, among other things, as an opportunity to grow new jobs. Yet in Wales and many other parts of Britain the problem was not only the loss of jobs, but the nature of those lost jobs. Coal mining and steel-making had been dangerous but were central to the British economy and at the heart of Welsh communities. When those jobs disappeared, the prospect of finding decent incomes for Welsh working men also ended. For more than forty years, twice as long as the Great Depression, the Valleys have not had enough jobs for those able to work, and the jobs that are available have been poorly paid. The first major phase of industrialisation gave birth to towns where almost 700,000 people continued to live despite the disappearance of the industries that brought their forefathers there. The second phase of factory work was short-lived but revolutionary in providing paid work for women. The workers in those towns were overwhelmingly working class in origin and occupation, daily facing dangers in the first phase that gave rise to new industrial organisations and radical aspirations which still endure. Industrialisation had saved the Welsh language from disappearing through out-migration and had moved the centre of gravity of the Welsh economy to the south. The end of industrialisation left Wales with over a thousand coal tips, many workers with outdated skills and a high proportion of people in poor health and poverty. UK Governments were content to see the European Union deal with the inherited problems, doing little themselves.

8

The Old Home Town

To be rooted is perhaps the most important and least
recognised need of the human soul.
Simone Weil (1949)

In 1967 a Welsh Office document announced: 'For both
economic and social reasons the Government reject any
policy which would assume the disintegration of the
substantial valley communities.' (*Wales the Way Ahead*).
Despite the boldness and vagueness of this declaration,
neither the UK Government nor, after devolution in
1998, the government based at Cardiff Bay has stemmed
the loss of jobs and people from valley towns. Newport
and Cardiff have each grown in recent years, mainly by
immigration from within Wales, while the coalfield
population has declined.

As major factories closed, it was assumed that the Valleys
would become dormitories with people daily travelling to
the jobs in Newport, Cardiff, Swansea and the M4 corridor.
Partly this has happened. But commuting by car cost money
that many in the Valleys did not have while commuting by
bus can take hours. And, often, workers from the Valleys
did not have the skills required by modern industry.
Scattered throughout the Valleys on council trading estates

or standing alone, small and medium-sized businesses provide work. But the number of jobs required to employ all those available to work seems beyond reach. A major reason is that for 700,000 people – equivalent to the combined populations of Newport, Cardiff and Swansea, and with 640,000 of these in the valleys feeding down to Newport and Cardiff – the Valleys are home. Sizeable towns, often with significant historical connections, are scattered throughout the area – Ammanford, Maesteg, Tonypandy, Porth, Pontypridd, Aberdare, Merthyr Tydfil, Ebbw Vale. The all-embracing link between collieries and the community may have gone, industrial jobs are no longer handed on from father to son, different generations of the same family often live far apart, but love of place, neighbourliness and fellow feeling remain defining characteristics. Newcomers notice it straightaway:

'People greet you in the street, even if you have never met. If you have met, however briefly, then you are in for a real chin-wag.'

'We have lovely neighbours and most people, unlike in London, are very friendly and happy to chat.'

(*Blaenau Gwent Voices*).

This is true but when homes across Britain are flooded, as increasingly they are, community spirit and neighbourly help appears in all the affected areas. The Covid-19 pandemic also provoked profound displays of human solidarity across Britain. These instinctive reactions to neighbours in distress, the belated recognition of those whose daily task it is to help others, were the opposite of everything represented by globalisation.

In good times as well as bad the Valleys retain, as many ex-mining communities do, a sense of community and caring for each other. For them 'society' does exist. There was a period in the 1980s when the closure of mines and factories through external forces – the Thatcher government, the development of global supply chains – brought a sense of impotence. People hoped and waited for help from central government. It was a time when, as the nationalist poet Harri Webb pungently wrote in his 'Anglomaniac Anthem':

> ... we're looking up England's arsehole
> Waiting for the manna to fall.

On the ground, local authorities, charitable organisations and volunteers combined to transform the physical landscape and develop new projects. The Valleys are greener and more pleasant to live in now than for the past 150 years.

Aberfan was a tragic wake-up call. On 21 October 1966, 144 people died when a colliery waste tip slid down the mountain side, engulfing Pantglas Junior School and killing 116 children. Many of the 1,200 coal tips in the Valleys have since been cleared or grassed-over. In 2002 the toxic Rechem plant at Pontypool was closed. At Abercwmboi in the Cynon valley, the phurnacite plant which closed in 1991 was notorious for its unhealthy, carcinogenic emissions into the local area. In 2005 122,000 tonnes of waste were removed from the site. Hidden dangers remain. Heavy rains and flooding caused by poor drainage and climate change threaten the stability of 350 old coal tips. A coal tip safety force was established after the Tylorstown landslide in February 2020. A new public body with responsibility for overseeing coal tip safety will be introduced in 2024.

Nonetheless, a combination of local authorities and private investors has attracted visitors to the Valleys. Festivals of various kinds proliferate. Hotels and meals have been improved. Private initiatives backed by local councils have produced Bike Park Wales at Abercanaid, 80,000 visitors a year with plans to expand; Rock UK, the climbing centre at Trelewis; Parkwood Outdoors at Dolygaer; and Zip World on the Rhigos mountain. They have joined the caves at Dan-yr-Ogof and the former slate quarries in Gwynedd as tourist attractions. An adventure holiday resort occupying 132 hectares is planned for the Afan Valley. Walking trails have appeared, railway tunnels that connected valleys and which have been closed for years are now seen as potential bicycle trails. The proposal to open the 1.4-mile-long Brunel designed Abernant tunnel which links Merthyr Tydfil and Aberdare is yet another example. Even longer is the 3,443-yard Rhondda Tunnel, the longest disused railway tunnel in Wales which links Blaencwm at the head of the Rhondda Fawr to Blaengwynfi in the Afan Valley. If the plans to open it as a cycle and walking trail succeed, it will be the longest in Europe. There are plans for a privately financed major leisure resort at Merthyr Tydfil with woodland lodges, a resort hotel, a tropical indoor water park, the UK's largest indoor snow centre and an Olympic-standard ski-slope. It is hoped to provide around 1,500 jobs in its construction and some 800 jobs when completed.

These initiatives are not just for tourists. They improve the experience of living in the Valleys. The notion is one of 'social prescribing'; walking and cycling in the open air as a way of improving health and beating depression. At Ynysybwl a Regeneration Partnership emphasises 'what we have, not what is wrong' and, Lottery funded, offers 'A Vision for our Valley'. In Penrhiwceiber local people raised money to reopen the local swimming pool. At Ferndale the local comprehensive school has taken the lead in regeneration activities. In January 2020 Treorchy High Street was named the best in the UK, a tribute to community-minded local entrepreneurs.

Heritage Attractions

Wales' history is now an attraction for tourists and an educational experience for the young. North Wales has attracted visitors since the eighteenth century to its mountains, to Port Meirion, to the steam railway from Porthmadog to Blaenau Ffestiniog, and in the Victorian era to the North Wales coastal resorts. The National Lottery Heritage Fund has since 1994 awarded over £430m to more than 3,100 history and heritage projects in every Welsh local authority area. The projects reflect every facet of Welsh history but not surprisingly there is increasing interest in the industrial history of Wales. There are now slate museums in North Wales. In the 1950s and 1960s, when the factories provided employment and the mines were still nationalised, many historic buildings were destroyed or allowed to rot away. They were seen as symbols of capitalist oppression. The iron-workers' cottages at Rhydycar, Merthyr Tydfil, dating from around 1800, which were threatened with destruction, can be seen at the open-air St Fagan's Museum near Cardiff where they have been reassembled and preserved. The pit ponies' stables in Dowlais were saved at the last minute. The triangle of workmen's cottages at Pentrebach, near Merthyr Tydfil, built in the late 1830s was not saved. The World Heritage Site at Blaenavon is now the place to go to experience and understand the former iron industry. Councils and social organisations, supported by Welsh Government, have turned former colliery sites into museums and country parks, such as the Dare Valley Park near Aberdare (the first such park created on reclaimed land in the UK), Penallta Country Park, the Cefn Coed Colliery Museum (Crynant), the Big Pit (Blaenafon), the Rhondda Heritage Park (Trehafod), the Parc Slip Nature Reserve (Tondu), and the South Wales Miners Museum in the Afan Valley at Cynonville.

The most ambitious scheme is at Merthyr Tydfil, the crucible of industrial Wales, where the sorely neglected furnaces at Cyfarthfa may yet be saved by a twenty-year £50m scheme by the Cyfarthfa Foundation, a charity which intends that the furnaces and Cyfarthfa Castle, home of the Crawshay dynasty, will become a major tourist attraction, portraying Merthyr's industrial and social history. The Cyfarthfa furnaces and the municipally owned Cyfarthfa Park, which contains the castle, former home of the Crawshay family, will be one historic site expanding from its current 160 acres to around 250 acres, becoming a heritage centre of international importance. Ian Ritchie Architects are leading the design. They have previously been involved in projects that include the famous glass pyramid at The Louvre, the 120m-high Spire in Dublin, and the glass lift towers at the Reina Sofia Museum of Modern Art at Madrid.

Also at Merthyr, the Foundation for Jewish Heritage has purchased the Grade II listed synagogue which is to become a Welsh Jewish Heritage Centre. Built from stone in 1872 in the Gothic Revival style, it is considered architecturally to be one of the most important synagogues in the UK. The Jewish community in Merthyr, which dated from the 1830s, was considerably strengthened at the end of the nineteenth century by refugees from the Russian and Polish pogroms whose families became prominent in Merthyr business and professions in the twentieth century. Major funding for the synagogue in the form of grants has been received from a variety of Jewish and heritage bodies.

Social Enterprises

Over 3,000 social enterprises operate in Wales employing around 55,000 people. This includes co-operatives, mutual organisations, local building societies, community interest companies, community-owned businesses, trading charities and individual social entrepreneurs. Often part-funded by Welsh Government grants, these organisations aim to make a profit but reinvest that surplus in developing skills, in cultural activities, in social or environmental causes or both, and by so doing contribute to the well-being goals of the Future Generations Act. They include the Principality, Swansea, and Monmouthshire building societies, Cwmpas (formerly the Wales Co-operative Centre), the Coalfields Regeneration Trust, Groundwork Wales, the Welsh Council for Voluntary Action, People and Work, UnLtd in Wales, Skyline, Canolfan Soar Merthyr Tydfil, and getting on for a score of Community Woodland Groups. The sector produced an aspirational document in 2020, *Transforming Wales Through Social Enterprise*, which set out a number of goals including a growth in the number of people engaging with social enterprises as customers, employees, volunteers or leaders between 2020 and 2030. The Welsh Government also is encouraging employee-owned businesses in Wales. In 2013 there were just 13. By May 2021 there were 37 and the Welsh Government aims to double that number to 74 by May 2026.

People and Work promotes education and learning as a means of tackling inequalities and promoting employment, as well as conducting research with a range of organisations. In both the Rhondda valleys it has promoted health and fitness schemes funded by the Rank Foundation as well as introducing around 400 young people to digital skills. A number have progressed into higher education or found paid work in the tech sector, important for the future of Welsh society and economy.

The UK exit from the European Union meant that EU

funding for 'hubs' that support local industries in Anglesey, Newtown, Carmarthen, Caerphilly and Wrexham ceased. All, except Wrexham, have secured alternative funding and there is hope that Wrexham will too. These 'hubs' provide office facilities, guidance, and networking opportunities for hundreds of local entrepreneurs, many of whom are self-employed.

Skyline, a project funded by the Friends Provident Foundation, initially ran from July 2018 to May 2019 and investigated the feasibility of giving a community control over the publicly owned landscape surrounding it. Most land in the Valleys is owned by local councils, the Coal Authority and the Welsh Government. The locations chosen for the study were Caerau, Treherbert and Ynysowen (Merthyr Vale and Aberfan). Five paid staff worked with local volunteers. The project established that if communities were given long leases over such land – 100 years or three to four generations – the key income-generating activities would be commercial forestry, hydro-electric energy generation and food production. These would provide jobs, entrepreneurial opportunities for new local businesses, and boost the local economy. Activities that could be part-funded by the money-making projects would be forest access for disabled people, general forestry path improvements and growing food such as salad and vegetables under glass or plastic heated by the hydro-electric projects. Although environmentally sound, these ideas did not promise many jobs. The Treherbert project has received Welsh Government funding to continue the experiment. These and similar initiatives, whether by private organisations, councils, charities or by volunteers, pronounce a revival of pride in locality and evidence that the desire to take back real control does exist.

But the Valleys need more than industrial museums, supportive 'hubs' and voluntary projects. In their impact upon jobs these various schemes echo the self-help schemes of the Great Depression. The measures described are imaginative, often necessary, but not sufficient. Despite everything the problems of the Valleys remain: unemployment, poor pay, low skills, mental and physical poor health. In November 2022, 100 people were made redundant at Garth Bakery in Abercynon. In October 2023 around 500 people were made redundant after UK Windows and Doors went into administration. It had sites in Treorchy, Llwynypia, Williamstown, and Taffs Well. Tillery Foods in Abertillery which employed 250 people went into administration in May 2023. There is a limit to what charities, volunteers and individual entrepreneurs can do. The population of the Valleys is declining as the young, particularly those with higher education, search for jobs elsewhere. Yet the Valleys are still home to hundreds of thousands of people. Access to jobs and, if possible, local jobs remains an urgent need.

New Jobs

The Welsh Government agency for tackling the Valleys' problems was the Valleys Taskforce set up in 2016. It was not as successful as initially hoped and was wound up on 31 March 2021. An assessment of its work concluded that its aims were too ambitious within the five-year period, and that it should have been better resourced. And, of course, progress was severely hampered by Covid-19. However, more than 700 new enterprises were set up and 3,300 additional jobs were created. The assessment is clear that further support and help for the Valleys communities is necessary.

Projects answering the Wales TUC call for 'Jobs Closer to Home' are part of the answer. The Global Centre of Rail Excellence, a centre for testing rail infrastructure and rolling stock, is at the 700 hectares Nant Helen opencast mining site at the head of the Dulais and Tawe valleys near Onllwyn. It straddles the local authority areas of Neath Port Talbot and Powys, partners in the £400m scheme with the Westminster Government contributing £20m and the Welsh Government £50m toward the first of three phases. Around 100 well-paid jobs will be created when the facility is completed with some hundreds more in the supply chain. Revenues of at least £20m a year are expected and it will collaborate with universities in Swansea, Cardiff and Birmingham on research and development. More than 100 firms have welcomed this world-class facility for rail research, testing and certification of rolling stock. Agreements have been reached with Transport for Wales and with Hitachi Rail to test the latest rail technology and develop the railways of tomorrow. Private capital is being sought to provide a hotel and a business technology park.

Ebbw Vale, designated as the Ebbw Vale Enterprise

Zone, is emerging as an important job centre for the Valleys after several false starts, including a motor racing track project that never materialised despite considerable expenditure. Around 600 well-paid jobs will come with the opening of a glass bottle manufacturing and recycling plant on the Rassau Industrial Estate. The bottles will go primarily to bottling plants in the UK, reducing the carbon footprint involved in travel. Simba Chain, an American tech company, has announced it will set up a base in Ebbw Vale providing 26 highly skilled jobs with an average salary of £60,000. Pulse Plastics Ltd is moving from Abercarn to a five-acre site in Ebbw Vale, creating around forty additional jobs. The Cardiff Capital Region has invested £2m equity into Apex Digital Technologies in Ebbw Vale and the global battery manufacturer GS Yuasa, already at Ebbw Vale, is increasing its labour force to around 460.

Ebbw Vale is also the site of the £20m National Digital Exploitation Centre (NDEC), the Valleys' response to the challenge of the technological revolution and an attempt to site the evolving new industries in a Valleys location. Set up by the Welsh Government's Tech Valleys Initiative in collaboration with Thales, the French multinational company, and the University of South Wales (Pontypridd), the NDEC is a research and education/training centre. It provides training in the latest digital technologies, and through its research laboratory, the opportunity to develop major digital advances or to test new digital concepts. It is a recognition of the need to update skills for the digital economy and an attempt to retain young people within the Valleys, a major problem. In May 2022 the £7m Resilient Works centre at Ebbw Vale was opened by the First Minister. It will enable tech companies to test and develop autonomous vehicle and power systems. The successful academic achievements of Valley schoolchildren are always a source of family pride. But too often those energetic, trained minds find job opportunities outside Wales. Through outreach training at Welsh colleges and universities, the NDEC aims to enable local people to move into well-paid high-tech jobs available at the new investments in Ebbw Vale.

A new 52,582 square-feet industrial unit completed in October 2023 is an £8.5m investment by the Welsh Government. It will be carbon neutral and provide space for manufacturing and service employments. It is a deliberate attempt to provide employment opportunities in the Valleys aided by the proximity of the dual carriageway A465. It is attracting strong interest. The costly and much criticised dualling of the originally three-lane A465 Heads of the Valleys road provides links for local business supply chains, tourism and leisure as well as for local residents. Originally conceived in the 1960s as a three-lane fast route for steel from Port Talbot to the car factories in the Midlands via the M50, it runs along the Heads of the Valleys with connections to Merthyr Tydfil, Rhymney, Tredegar, Ebbw Vale and Brynmawr. It was a factor in bringing factories to the Heads of the Valleys towns, such as the Convatec site at Rhymney employing over 100 people, and recently has helped to bring the bottling plant to Ebbw Vale.

It is also a fast route for people from the English Midlands to travel to Pembrokeshire and Ireland or, by connecting with the A470, to enter the Brecon Beacons National Park. Opportunities for heritage tourism exist in the ironworks remains along the Heads of the Valleys. In addition to those at the World Heritage Site at Blaenavon and the Cyfarthfa project, the remains at Clydach, Sirhowy, Ebbw Vale, Tredegar, Rhymney and Hirwaun, with improved signage and access, could make the A465 a heritage route linking the Clydach Gorge to Neath Abbey.

At Merthyr Tydfil a new industrial park is being built at the former site of the ICI works at Pant. When completed, it will provide fourteen factory units but the Valleys are not the only sites away from the coasts where jobs are being created. In the UK the second fastest-growing area for businesses with fewer than ten employees is just outside the Valleys in Torfaen County Borough with headquarters at Cwmbran. In mid-Wales the Welsh Government, in partnership with Carmarthenshire County Council, is supporting the construction of high-quality commercial office space at Cross Hands. The European Regional Development Fund is providing £2.4m towards the cost. At Llandrindod Wells the vehicle firm, Riversimple Movement Ltd., makes progress towards producing hydrogen-fuelled motor vehicles. It has a collaboration agreement with tech giant Siemens and a £2m grant from the Welsh Government. At Knighton, Wales' leading soft drinks company, Radnor Hills, has invested £7m in its headquarters there and is taking on more staff. In Welshpool the Invertek Drives company, which manufactures electric motor control technology, is investing £6m in an expansion. At Ceredigion, market-research company Delineate is basing its headquarters there with fifty employees. Potential employment sites at Aberystwyth, Newtown and Brecon are being investigated. Industrial employment in North Wales is in good health (see page 116). Foundational Economy ideas are being developed throughout Wales (Chapter 12).

Lessons from the Pandemic

Covid-19 illuminated the significance of community and the importance of looking after the people and places where thousands live. It also revealed that many of the poorly paid were doing essential work. The TUC estimated in 2020 that over 456,000 workers in Wales, nearly half a million, were paid less than £10 per hour. They include 38 per cent of the key workers in Wales, almost four in ten. A majority are women. A prime example is care homes where a high proportion of workers do not earn the living wage, turnover is high and numbers are known to leave for work in supermarkets where they are paid the living wage. Like hospital workers, those in care homes were most at risk of catching the virus. Many did. An ageing population means that care workers are in a growth industry but one that is largely funded out of declining and over-stretched public budgets. The eventual answer will be a National Care Service akin to the National Health Service and working in tandem with it.

Covid-19 also exposed and emphasised the inequalities in health that have existed for generations in Rhondda Cynon Taf, Merthyr Tydfil, Blaenau Gwent and Neath Port Talbot. The first three areas were consistently the most affected in Wales by Covid-19, a consequence of past employments and current poverty, but also of neighbourliness with friends or different generations of the same family living close together, often in the same street. Research by Bambra, Munford, Brown, et al. show that improving health in former English coalfield towns would significantly improve productivity and wages. This research has lessons for Wales where the inherited problems are even greater. Better health and well-being should be measurements of economic success.

There is a related issue. Britain was unprepared. Never again must we be unprepared when a pandemic invades or recurs, as is more than possible. It is vital that there should be UK access to personal protective equipment (PPE) rather than depending on overseas resources. During the pandemic, high-quality PPE equipment was manufactured at the Royal Mint at Llantrisant and by firms based in Cardiff, Neath, Ystrad Mynach, Ystalyfera, Kenfig and Clydach, among others. Medical visors, scrubs and face masks were supplied to the NHS, care homes and councils. A laboratory within Rhondda Cynon Taf produced coronavirus antibody testing kits. At Newport a Covid-19 laboratory tested specimens. In Crumlin a diagnostic firm won an order for one million rapid Covid-19 antibody tests. In Wrexham a major pharmaceutical company was involved in mass production of a Covid-19 vaccine. The lesson has not been overlooked. Production of PPE equipment at Kenfig Hill is now on a permanent basis while at Rhymney the US firm Innova Medical will initially employ 300 workers producing Covid-19 test kits. Further employment on the site is expected from the production of non-Covid testing products. These are arresting examples of how flexible firms can be when the need is urgent. But rebuilding the British and particularly the Welsh economy will require much more.

9

Railways

Travel broadens the mind.
Proverbs

The Welsh Government does not control most of the railways in Wales. This is because the Welsh Government did not have the confidence to take on that responsibility. As the confidence of the Welsh Government has grown over the years, that decision is recognised as a serious mistake, a mistake the Scottish Government did not make. Westminster has never allowed the Welsh Government to revisit that decision. One consequence has been that the HS2 rail line which will run from London to Birmingham is classified as one which benefits Wales although not one inch of the line enters Wales. Scotland and Northern Ireland receive payments from Westminster every time a tunnel is dug or a length of rail is laid for HS2 in England; Wales gets nothing. If the line was classified as an England-only project, Wales would receive at least £2bn. It is an issue which in Wales is felt by many to be deeply unjust. The cancellation in 2023 of the HS2 line between Birmingham and Manchester further weakened the argument used by Westminster that the line helped

Welsh travellers because of the geographical proximity of the two countries. In compensation the Prime Minister, Rishi Sunak, pledged to electrify the North Wales railway line using £1bn saved. This statement was made without prior consultation with Network Rail or the Welsh Government. No date has been given when that work will commence and there is no public breakdown of the anticipated costs.

Meanwhile the Great Western Partnership – an alliance of public, private and third-sector stakeholders in South Wales and south-west England – has said that an investment of between £1bn and £2bn would bring more frequent and faster journey times to an area that has cross-border strengths in aerospace, green energy, cyber and creative sectors. In the longer term, up to 2050, the partnership has a range of proposals for closer working that would cost between £7bn and £8bn.

The Metro

Wales is, however, responsible for the Metro, the twenty-first century answer to getting people to their work, a system of electric trams/trains running on the historic railway system that links the central and eastern valleys to Cardiff and Newport. In 2018 Keolis Amey was awarded a fifteen-year rail franchise for Wales and the Borders. Then Covid-19 happened. Reduced passenger numbers and a huge fall in revenue meant that a commercial franchise was no longer possible. As the Operator of Last Resort under the Railways Act (1993) the Welsh Government agency Transport for Wales stepped in to run the franchise and manage the contracts entered into by Keolis Amey.

Work to electrify 170 kilometres of Valleys' track began in August 2020 but Covid-19 delayed the project. The new tram-trains were tested in 2023 with expectation that when fully operational journey times would be cut and the frequency of trains would increase. As part of the scheme, car parks at Valley stations were enlarged. The scheme will electrify and upgrade the core railway routes connecting Treherbert, Aberdare and Merthyr Tydfil to Cardiff and Ebbw Vale to Newport. At peak times these connections will run four times every hour while tri-mode trains, which can switch between diesel, electric and battery modes, will travel on the Rhymney and Coryton lines. Pontypridd will have twelve services into Cardiff in both directions. Covid-19 and inflation have pushed the cost of the Metro up from the initial estimate of £738m to around £1bn. The original budget included £164m from the European Union which was conditional upon the whole scheme being completed by 2023. Delays caused by Covid-19 will extend that deadline. Trying to upgrade all trains in three years has been a major problem with Covid delaying the delivery of new trains. Old two-carriage trains were still in use in 2023 between Cardiff and Manchester. In October 2023 the Welsh Government increased its grant to Transport for Wales to £125m, an increase of more than 50 per cent, because passenger growth had not grown as expected. Without that cash injection, rail services and jobs would have been cut.

Improvements to bus and rail services in and around Newport are seen as the answer to the M4 congestion in the south-east corner of Wales. One answer, likely to proceed, would be to create new rail stations between Cardiff and the Severn Tunnel at Cardiff East, Newport West, Somerton, Llanwern, and Magor and Undy. There are separate plans for a mainline station at St Mellons. The UK Government will have to finance the stations as the line is not devolved. Transport for Wales also has responsibility for bus transport. Integrating the currently inadequate bus services with the rail network would result in electronic ticketing across both systems, similar to London's Oyster. The intention is to have one integrated Welsh network where multiple tickets will not be required and dependence on car journeys will be reduced. The development of this all-Wales vision depends, however, upon the development of a Metro scheme in North Wales and the collaboration of the UK Government.

The headquarters of Transport for Wales (TfW) at Pontypridd replaces the former one in Cardiff. It is expected to house 500 TfW staff. A graduate training programme is part of this development. How many of these will be new jobs is not clear. The Pontypridd headquarters is in addition to the £100m depot at Taffs Well which employs approximately 500 people as train crews, maintenance and control centre staff. To cope with the new timetables, an additional 200 train drivers are receiving two years' training. The Metro will certainly have a major impact upon the South Wales economy, enabling easier travelling across the whole area, while encouraging more local commuting and shopping, especially if the ticket prices include off-peak deals. By providing more jobs and swifter access to job opportunities in Newport and Cardiff, the Metro is part of the answer to sustaining Valley towns.

10

Tools for the Job

'Come to Wales, we're very cheap' is *not* something this government is prepared to consider.

Mark Drakeford

It is easy to forget how recently the Welsh Government acquired powers in certain areas to act independently of the UK Government. The National Assembly for Wales was established in 1999 as a directly elected sixty-member body with four key roles: to represent Wales and its people; to make laws for Wales; to agree certain Welsh taxes; and to hold the Welsh Government to account. It was not until the referendum in 2011 and the subsequent Wales Act (2014) that the Welsh Government acquired some primary law-making powers and was able to move from a largely administrative role to a much more ambitious one.

Devolution eventually brought to the Assembly, now the Senedd, a wide range of responsibilities. They include economic, industrial and social development, education and training, the NHS in Wales, agriculture, forestry, fishing and food, local government, housing, social services, transport, planning and the environment, arts, culture and the Welsh language. In addition the Senedd has acquired tax-raising powers. In April 2008 it acquired the ability to raise a landfill tax and land transaction tax, and in April 2019 it acquired powers to set council tax and business rates, and to vary income tax rates. Its income tax powers have yet to be used. Its revenue from taxes is around £5bn. Despite these wide-ranging powers, Brexit, Covid-19 with its variants, and the determination of the Westminster Government to play a dominating role mean that the government in Cardiff has by no means a free hand to address Wales' many social and economic problems. Welsh intentions have been set out in policy documents the most important of which is the Well-being of Future Generations Act (2015).

The six ambitious goals of this Act underpin all the economic and social developments in Wales emanating from the Welsh Government. The goals aim to improve the economic, social and environmental well-being of Wales: to make Wales prosperous, resilient, wealthier, more equal, with cohesive communities and a vibrant culture with a thriving Welsh language. The fundamental questions behind this Act are: 'What are we doing now to improve Wales over the next fifty years?', 'What will we do to make Wales a better place?' It was an Act that made Wales the first country in the world to enshrine sustainable development principles into public decision-making.

As part of the Act and to help its implementation, two institutions were created. The first was that each local authority in Wales should have a Public Service Board. Each Board contains members of the local authority, the local health board, the Welsh Fire and Rescue Authority, and the National Resources Body for Wales. It may also invite Welsh Ministers, the relevant Chief Constable and Crime Commissioner, and representatives from at least one body representing local voluntary organisations. Each authority must produce annually a local Well-being Plan after wide consultations. These Boards with their plans are important for involving public services and ideas in the development of local economies. The second institution was the post of Future Generations Commissioner. The task of the Commissioner is to promote sustainable development principles and to encourage public bodies, particularly the Welsh Government, to take account of the long-term impact of decisions. The Commissioner has initiated discussions on a wide range of topics including housing, transport, the education and skills required for the future, the treatment for mental health, the impact of adverse childhood experiences, the possible consequences of planning decisions, and the introduction of a basic income.

It is against the background of this far-seeing Act that Welsh Government economic and social strategies have been developed. *Prosperity for All* (2017) and the *Economic Action Plan* (December 2017) emphasised the economic priorities for the years up to 2021. *Economic Resilience and Reconstruction Mission* published in February 2021 set out proposals to recover from the effects of the pandemic. The first of these documents, influenced by the Dickens Report, introduced the concept of public investment with a social purpose or 'Something for Something'. It required businesses that receive financial support from the Welsh Government to commit to growth, fair work, reducing their carbon footprint, and promoting health and learning in the workplace. Whilst more than 200 businesses signed the contract, the Welsh Government intends that this social partnership model shall become statute law through a Social Partnership Act. Most of the public loans and grants that private businesses receive come from the Development Bank of Wales, one of the largest equity investors in the UK, with over 1,000 business customers and a financial pot of £500m to aid firms investing in Wales. It is wholly owned by the Welsh Government.

The *Economic Action Plan* focused on place – 'places matter' – and accepted the concept of the Foundational Economy, (discussed in Chapter 12), which has general application throughout Wales but is most important in those areas where the local economy lacks private investment. *Economic Resilience* emphasised the importance of training and skills, the green and circular economy, and research and development. Those strategies are discussed in Chapter 13. The Welsh Government also published in 2019 its *National Plan: Future Wales* which set out a series of aspirations with advice and guidance to local authorities and other bodies on how to work towards achieving the plan. Altogether, the *Well-being Act*, *Prosperity for All*, the *Action Plan*, the *Economic Resilience* paper, *Future Wales*, and *Fair Work Wales*, set out a bold and ambitious framework for economic renewal.

Delayed Delivery

Has it been delivered? It has not. Covid-19 followed by very slow growth have been substantial impediments but not the only reasons. The aspirations depend on a high level of co-operation between the Welsh Government, private investors, twenty-two local authorities, the City Deals discussed below and, not least, the Westminster Government. These relationships mean that the Welsh Government does not have an entirely free hand. As Professor Kevin Morgan has pointed out, while the quality of government is most important for creating an environment that fosters rather than impedes economic development, what is crucially important is the quality of inter-government relationships across the UK. The relationship with Westminster has become increasingly difficult since Brexit and the passing of the Internal Market Act, mentioned earlier.

A major problem has been the clear gap between the original responsibilities of the Assembly when it was first set up, the Senedd's current expanded responsibilities and aspirations, and its ability to fulfil them. The Senedd is too small. The Northern Ireland Assembly has 90 members, one for every 20,690 citizens; the Scottish Assembly has 129 members, one for every 41,897 citizens; in Wales the Senedd, with 60 members, has one member for every 51,887 citizens. When ministers and those with official duties are taken out, only 41 members remain to monitor legislation. The number of support staff is consequently also inadequate. The small size of the Senedd affects its ability to deal with urgent problems. The Electoral Reform Society has calculated that the cost of 30 new Senedd members would be more than covered by the costs of losing four members of the European Parliament as a result of Brexit and the loss of eight MPs as a result of forthcoming constituency boundary changes. In May 2022 it was announced that the Welsh Government and Plaid Cymru had agreed that the Senedd would increase by 36 members before the next Senedd elections in 2026, taking the total of members to 96. The electoral system proposed has been severely criticised by various commentators as being needlessly expensive and one where voters are deprived of choice. Instead of voting for individual candidates, voters will be required to vote for a political party. This means that Independent candidates, those not standing as members of a political party, will not be allowed to stand. Successful candidates will then be chosen by party leaders instead of by voters. The proposed voting system gives more power to political parties and takes away from individual voters a choice they have had since the introduction of the universal franchise in 1928.

In preparation for the future, the Welsh Government will introduce before its current term is ended two new taxes. One will be a revision of council tax, last reviewed in Wales in 2003. England and Scotland have not revised their council tax levels since they were first introduced in 1993. The second will be a tourism tax paid by people staying in commercially let, overnight visitor accommodation. Local authorities will decide whether to introduce a levy and the funds raised will be used to improve local areas. The earliest a visitor levy can be introduced will be 2027. Tourism taxes are common in Europe. The necessary building blocks are also being put in place for the establishment of a national care service for Wales which will be free at the point of need. A national office for care and support will be established in April 2024. Also in April 2024 the Commission for Tertiary Education and Research will be created. It will be second only to the Welsh NHS in budget terms and will be the first in the UK to have a single overarching authority for tertiary education, overseeing further education, higher education, sixth forms, apprentices, and adult community learning.

What Matters Most

Meanwhile there is the fundamental question: what do people actually want in their daily lives? In June 2020 public demonstrations and a 24,000-signature petition caused the local health board to reverse its decision to close the Royal Glamorgan Hospital Accident and Emergency Department at Ynysmaerdy. The fears and hopes of people affected by the original decision were ignored until it became impossible to do so. Additional resources were found to keep the Accident and Emergency Department open. It is an illuminating lesson. Answers to problems should not be handed down from above but discussed and agreed with those who are affected by them and who have to live with the consequences. It has been the practice in Britain recently for governments to ask people for their opinion on legislation already proposed. The Welsh Government does so regularly. It is a recognition that neither the man nor the woman in Whitehall, nor even in Cardiff, always knows best. But it is not the same as asking people what they want. The Welsh Government and now the Westminster Government have at times asked local authorities what local actions they would recommend. This is a step further but it is still not the same as asking the people. A relevant example is the imposition of 20 mph upon vehicles in urban areas. Public reaction is resulting in a modification of the rules in certain areas.

Before the pandemic, the Valley Taskforce did ask people in the Valleys what mattered most to them. The foremost answers were public services, public transport, open spaces, jobs and the skills to do them, health, and 'my community'. In February 2021 PricewaterhouseCoopers (PwC) polled UK residents on how to reduce inequalities. The priorities that people in Wales voted for were: affordable housing 66 per cent, good-paying jobs 55 per cent, investment in high streets and town centres 48 per cent, good public services 43 per cent, and education and skills 41 per cent. In both cases housing, good jobs and pay, skills, public services, my community/town centres, appear consistently. Not surprisingly, health is a Valleys' priority. These are the people's priorities yet too many in Wales and the UK live without them. Their provision by Westminster or by Cardiff would be welcome. Actions will speak louder than all the words spent on constitutional wrangles.

It is increasingly apparent that in the twenty-first century, reform must come from a process in which the needs of the people are understood and accepted by governments as a basis for action. Policy decisions should reflect public preferences. The Carnegie UK Trust is clear: 'Well-being cannot be "done to" people, it has to be done by and with them.' Citizens' Assemblies are being used in a variety of countries, Canada, Denmark, Poland, Belgium, Ireland and Scotland among them. They are the means by which the voice of those directly affected can be heard and, whenever possible, their decisions implemented. Citizens' Assemblies consist of a cross-section of the public, randomly selected, and usually numbering 50 to 100. Through study, discussion, argument, and sometimes through questioning experts on the subject being considered, they arrive at a recommendation to the government. This would really be taking back control.

The State we are in

For two centuries Wales industrialised and then it de-industrialised, leaving behind large numbers of unemployed people in the densely populated Valleys and North Wales coastal towns. Nonetheless in the north and south, near Wrexham, Newport, Cardiff and Swansea, there are important centres of work in new expanding industries and services. Businesses are growing in mid-Wales. Wales exports electricity and water to England. The Metro will provide faster travel between the Valleys and the coast. Despite setbacks, the Cardiff government is committed to creating a national network of banks – Banc Cambria – providing investment and advice to the

265,000 small and medium-sized firms in Wales and an everyday banking service for all regardless of income or wealth. Such a bank would give local economies a fresh sense of purpose. In 2024 the Commission for Tertiary Education and Research in Wales will be launched; the second largest public body in Wales, second only to the NHS. Its task is to provide a system of technical education and work-based learning that relates to today's and tomorrow's advanced technologies. In 2027 courses will begin for the new Vocational Certificate of Secondary Education which will be available for pupils who wish to take these new work and skills qualifications alongside or instead of the General Certificate of Education. All learners, whatever their aptitude, interest or ability, will gain recognition for what they know and can do.

On the other hand, the NHS is in crisis, thousands of children live in poverty, local councils are threatened by bankruptcy, skilled workers are in short supply, thousands of workers at the Port Talbot steelworks will become unemployed, and the Welsh Government believes it is owed at least £2bn by the Westminster Government.

National renewal is a long-term task which needs a willingness by local authorities, the private sector, and the Westminster and Welsh Governments to work together. It requires different departments within local authorities to work together, which is not always the case. It requires time for innovative solutions learned in a largely post-industrial society to be applied. But time is running out. Rachel Carson's prophetic book *Silent Spring* was published as long ago as 1962.

FUTURE WALES

11

The Urgent Challenge

It is time for the Government to implement these
changes with the urgency that the science demands.
The Climate Change Committee (2021)

The year 2023 was the hottest across the world since
records began in 1884. Climate change is usually seen
as the threat to life on this planet, but it is caused by the
way we live. Changing the way we live will not be easy
and the time in which to do it is short. The everyday
changes to the world's climate can be seen in the acid
rain that poisons lakes, the carbon dioxide killing coral
reefs, the episodes of unbearable heat in Asia and the
Middle East, droughts, grass and forest fires in Canada,
Australia, Greek islands, the USA and the UK, in floods
and loss of life in Germany and Belgium, landslides and
unstable coal tips in South Wales. The rise in sea levels
caused by huge ice sheets melting at the North and South
Poles will put low-lying countries and cities under water,
forcing people to migrate to dry land. This rise in sea
levels may be irreversible. The average surface
temperature over land areas in the Arctic in 2020 was
the highest since records began in 1900. More widely
the global surface temperature has increased faster since

1970 than in any other 50-year period over the past 2,000 years. Limiting the increase in global temperature to 1.5°C requires CO_2 emissions to fall by 65 per cent by 2035 and 99 per cent by 2050. The Intergovernmental Panel on Climate Change Actions claims that actions taken during the 2020s will have impacts for thousands of years. In Wales the current estimate is that over 11 per cent of its land is at risk of flooding from the sea or rivers with 22,000 properties a risk. More than £214m is being spent by the Welsh Government over 2022 to 2025 to manage the flooding linked to climate change.

Maps released by Natural Resources Wales show that considerable areas of Newport, Cardiff, Barry and Swansea could be under water by 2050 if nothing is done. Cardiff is ranked sixth in the world in danger from the effects of climate change. Canton, Grangetown and Riverside in Cardiff are particularly vulnerable to river flooding. Also at risk of flooding are Maindee in Newport, Llandudno, Prestatyn, Rhyl, and Llanelli. In West Wales £32m is being spent to protect Aberaeron from rising sea levels. In North Wales parts of the A55, the coastal railway and holiday resorts will also be flooded. Fairbourne in Gwynedd is liable to be submerged by mid-century. Altogether 245,000 homes are at risk of flooding. The Welsh Government has warned planners to consider current and future coastal erosion risks. New developments of homes, schools, hospitals and emergency services must avoid the areas at risk. The signs are clear. Rising sea levels threaten coastal towns while heavy rainfalls threaten the stability of tips in South

Wales, releasing thousands of cubic metres of rock and debris causing damage to trees, sewers and threatening houses.

An urgent inspection of all coal tips in Wales was undertaken by the Coal Authority with the Welsh Local Government Association, local authorities and Natural Resources Wales, to assess any risk to people or property. With 2,144 tips Wales has more than 40 per cent of all the coal tips in the UK with 294 classed as 'high risk': 64 in Rhondda Cynon Taf, 59 in Merthyr Tydfil, 70 Caerphilly, 42 Bridgend, 16 in Blaenau Gwent, 35 in Neath Port Talbot and 8 in Swansea. A database of the tips in the South Wales coalfield exists along with a helpline. This is no longer sufficient. In 2021 the Law Commission reported that the laws governing coal tips in Wales, set up after the Aberfan disaster, were outdated and inadequate to deal with the legacy of industrialisation. New legislation was needed to avert dangers and enable remedial work to be carried out. In May 2022 final recommendations on changes in the law were made to the Welsh Government. A new supervisory body will ensure the safety of coal tips. All tips will be given a safety category on a scale of one to five. Those categorised as one will be inspected every six months and appraised every year. A new national asset register will be set up and there will be a requirement for inspections and remedial works to be carried out. If not, civil sanctions will be applied. The UK Government has insisted that the cost of making these tips safe, estimated to be £600m over ten to fifteen years, must be paid by the Welsh Government despite the tips being created before devolution and the coal produced by Welsh pits fuelling the nineteenth-century expansion of the British Empire.

Action Needed Now

These safety issues are just part of a much greater problem. More than 300 organisations in Wales have called for greater legal protection for nature. Wales is the only nation in the UK which has not created an independent body to oversee the implementation of environmental laws. The release of the Report of the Intergovernmental Panel on Climate Change (IPCC) in August 2021 said that beyond doubt human activity was changing the Earth's climate in 'unprecedented' ways. Some of the changes are now inevitable and 'irreversible'. Only rapid and drastic reductions in greenhouse gases would prevent global heating rising to 1.5°C above the present level leading to an acceleration of climate breakdown. That will mean exhausting heatwaves, devastating droughts, world-wide flooding and mass migration. This report largely corroborated evidence given earlier in 2021 to the Welsh Government by the Climate Change Committee (CCC), an independent statutory body set up by the UK's Climate Change Act (2008). It advises the UK and devolved governments on preparing and adapting to the threat of climate change. Its 2021 report on the UK and Wales spelt out the threat to life on Earth and stressed that the decade 2021 to 2031 will be *decisive* for tackling climate change. The

IPCC Report was acknowledged by governments world-wide but progress in the UK and elsewhere is slow and inadequate. Dr Camilla Kingdon, President of the Royal College of Paediatrics and Child Health, has warned of the 'grave risk' to children of the climate emergency. Physical and mental health is being affected, she claimed, with children in lower-income families at the greatest risk.

The UN Climate Change Conference (COP27) held in Sharm el-Sheikh, Egypt, in November 2022 agreed that a fund would be set up within the next year to rebuild the physical and social infrastructure of countries ravaged by extreme weather events. It seemed a major step forward but there was no agreement on how much money should be paid in, by whom, and on what basis. A resolution passed at the previous conference in Glasgow a year earlier that global emissions would peak by 2025 was dropped. Based on current commitments the goal of confining temperature rises to 1.5°C is out of reach. There is a huge gap between the pledges made at successive conferences and the actions being taken.

Wales Must Do More

Taking action to prevent the worst of climate changes can mean more jobs, cleaner air, quieter transport, more energy-efficient homes and a more equitable society. In March 2021 the Welsh Government announced a transport strategy aimed at reducing carbon emissions which made up 17 per cent of these emissions in Wales. The intention is to increase the number of non-car journeys from the current 32 per cent to 45 per cent by 2045. The increase will come from more journeys on foot, by bicycle and on public transport. More than £210m has been invested by the Welsh Government in cycle routes, trains and buses across Wales. The Welsh Government is also committed to building in its current term 20,000 new homes for social rent that will be entirely carbon neutral and will consume less power than they produce. There is more than some doubt as to whether this will be achieved in the current timescale.

In June 2021 the Welsh Government set up a Ministry for Climate Change which brought together housing, energy, the environment, planning and transport under one ministry. Climate change and its consequences are now at the heart of Welsh Government decision-making. The target is that the public sector will be carbon neutral by 2030. By 2050 the aim is a 100 per cent reduction in carbon emissions into the atmosphere (net zero) from all sources.

One of the first actions of the new ministry was to suspend all new road building, except for the Llandeilo bypass and completion of the A465, until there has been a review of alternative ways of spending the money. The speed limit in all built-up areas is now 20 mph, although this will be reviewed. In March 2023 the Environment (Air Quality and Soundscapes) (Wales) Bill was introduced which gives the Welsh Government greater ability to tackle air and noise pollution that impacts upon human health, biodiversity and the natural environment. It received general support as a major step towards a greener, fairer and healthier future. These are just the first of what will be difficult but necessary actions if climate change is, at the least, mitigated.

A June 2023 report from the Climate Change Committee, the UK's independent adviser on tackling climate change, argued that Wales is not doing enough to meet its targets. Whilst praising the recycling of waste, efforts which 'remain higher than in the rest of the UK', and noting the positive steps taken to cancel major road projects on environmental grounds, the report said that Wales needs to do more. In particular it needs to deliver a widespread electric vehicle charging network; decarbonise public buildings, social housing and fuel-poor homes; develop a detailed plan for delivering energy-efficient measures and low-carbon heat, including investment costs; and address the funding gap for environmental support.

12

Building on what we have

For twenty years we've pretended we know what we're doing on the economy – and the truth is we don't really know what we're doing on the economy. Nobody knows what they are doing on the economy... Everybody is making it up as we go along... we need to try a different approach.
Lee Waters (25 June, 2019)

This uninhibited comment by a Welsh Government minister raised eyebrows yet it was true that for more than two decades Wales had had the lowest Gross Value Added (GVA) per head of any region or country in the UK. Behind Waters' frank statement lay the fact that industrialisation has been about shareholder value and not about Abertillery, Blaenafon, the Rhondda, Gwauncaegurwen or Blaenau Ffestiniog. When the mines, factories and quarries have gone and the roller coaster is back at the bottom, these are not places where footloose factories are likely to settle. They can choose anywhere in the world.

What is needed is focused local action. The umbilical link between the local economy and the local community that existed for over 200 years has seemingly been broken. Can that link be re-established? The former industries no longer exist but in the Valleys and throughout Wales the components of life as we know it – the essential infrastructure of our civilisation – water, food, energy, houses, health, roads and railways, internet connections, schools and colleges, childcare, retail banking, local shops and services, the cables, pipes and networks that connect us to services, are still there. To these, increased leisure has added libraries, open spaces and parks. The providers of these necessary services exist all around us: shop assistants and stackers of shelves, care workers, cleaners, doctors and nurses, local builders and market-stall holders, lorry and bus drivers, teachers and postmen, librarians and bank clerks. They are the people who make life possible, sometimes literally possible. In Wales these jobs are more than 40 per cent of total employment. The goods and services they provide are essential to the local population. Yet until Covid-19 these local services and their workers were taken for granted. We were blinded by the neo-liberal argument that the value of these goods and services was decided in the marketplace. The pandemic taught that life matters more than wealth. Those who do the essential jobs *are* essential.

The Anchor Institutions

The employers of these essential workers are 'anchor institutions'. They include local councils, the further education colleges, the medical practitioners and hospitals of the National Health Service, residential care homes, the police, the universities, housing associations, garages, post offices, banks and building societies, local contractors, private shops and markets, small and medium-sized firms, delivery firms, community centres. They account for at least one in every three pounds we spend. They are essential to our lives and also important providers of jobs and incomes. There are also local services that are not essential to our lives but which we have come to expect and felt their absence during the lockdowns: barbers and hairdressers, coffee shops, furniture and clothing shops.

To look at local economies in this way reveals employments that we hardly think about but which demonstrate a clear and essential link between jobs and the community. Since the collapse of mining and the flight of transnational firms, these 'unseen' jobs have been crucial in communities that otherwise would have died. This is the 'Every-day Economy' or 'Foundational Economy'. An understanding and appreciation of the Foundational Economy had begun to grow before the pandemic and a valuable introduction is in *When Nothing Works* published by Manchester University Press, 2023. The Welsh Government had already committed itself to this new approach to increase wealth across Wales and keep it there. Brexit increased its salience.

The Foundational Economy builds communities from the bottom up. Local employers who provide essential services exist where they are because that is where people are. Every town in Wales has a Foundational Economy that can be fostered and encouraged. In developing the Foundational Economy, there are five broad principles that can be applied although not to a full extent in every locality. Each principle is a means to improving local wealth and retaining it within the locality.

Five Principles

1. Support local businesses

Wherever possible, local councils, hospitals, colleges, universities and businesses should sign contracts with local suppliers and by this means increase local jobs, retain wealth locally and shorten supply chains. Goods and services produced by local people strengthen social relationships and boost local incomes. There is considerable scope for action. Professor Dylan Jones-Evans has noted that 'the 22 local authorities in Wales have a revenue expenditure of £8bn (excluding debt financing costs) and £1.5bn in capital expenditure'. At present there is no evidence how much is spent in Wales. Although 'construction contracts with a total value of £1.94bn have been awarded to Welsh public bodies since 2015, only 17.1 per cent of the total value was awarded to firms with a Welsh-registered address.' (*Western Mail*, 8 February 2020). The Federation of Small Businesses confirms that for every £1 local authorities spend on goods and services with local small and medium-sized employers, an additional 63p is generated for the local economy. Buying from local providers boosts local development. Around 48 per cent of NHS Wales' £22m food budget is spent outside Wales. Wherever possible, it should be replaced by local spending, retaining income in Wales and supporting local and regional economies.

2. Fair employment

End the low pay and insecurity of those who provide essential services: the carers, porters, cleaners, refuse workers, those who carry and deliver. These are tasks with social and economic meaning, although it took the pandemic to demonstrate their essential nature. Social care is the seventh largest employment sector in Wales contributing £2.2bn to the Welsh economy. A first step, where they are employed by the state or local councils, is to pay the Living Wage to those workers who do not receive it. Where training would be necessary or helpful, it should be provided. Parts of the social care sector in Wales have a 30 per cent annual turnover of the workforce, which is both extremely costly and bad for the quality of service. Where these services are under-staffed, an increase in the number of jobs would support local employment and increase local spending.

3. Develop local ownership

Encourage locally owned businesses, whether privately owned, employee owned, or in municipal ownership. Rents are low in most of Wales compared with city locations. Build relationships between local businesses so that the income of these businesses circulates locally instead of going to distant shareholders. A sub-group of the Valleys Taskforce encouraged small and medium-sized firms to take forward this approach but also to explore opportunities for export business. One of the prime weaknesses of Wales' industrial structure is that too few small businesses grow to medium-sized or even into large businesses.

4. Local use of land

Develop and extend community management and use of public sector land and facilities. Much of the land in Wales is owned by the Forestry Commission, local authorities, the Coal Authority, and the Senedd. Community management could lead to energy generation, food growing and commercial forestry. The businesses and the income derived would boost the local community. There is a view that winding up the Land Authority for Wales, which was consolidating ownerships to public benefit, was a mistake and that it should be brought back.

5. Circulate and invest local wealth

Encourage and increase investment from local sources of investment such as credit unions, local authority pension funds, and mutually owned building societies such as the Swansea, Principality, or Monmouthshire societies, so that the wealth that exists in the locality is circulated and the need for outside capital is reduced.

Investing in Communities

These are unconventional principles. They emphasise building from the bottom up rather than relying upon imported businesses. They recognise the significance of *social* rather than individual consumption of goods and services. The primary purpose of policy therefore becomes ensuring the supply of basic services, whether public or private, to all citizens. The principles are based upon place and the growth and circulation of wealth within that place. They are about investing in people and well-being and making communities stronger and more resilient.

They are about taking back control and dispelling the disappointment, distrust and disempowerment felt by so many faced with boarded-up shops and closed bank branches; 87 per cent of deprived areas in Wales are in South Wales. The Valleys, where private investment is weak, stand out as suitable places for treatment but it is a strategy that is being applied throughout Wales. There is clear evidence that people wish to participate in decisions that affect them.

By their nature many jobs in the Foundational Economy suffer from low productivity, low skills and low pay. 'Austerity' deprived local authorities of funds for more than a decade with the effect that most are unable to employ specialists with the managerial expertise and knowledge that could tackle these issues. The Welsh Government's strategy is to test how far local economies can build upon what already exists and, through learning by experiment, discover what is possible and effective. In 2019 it set up a £4.5m Foundational Economy Challenge Fund to support projects by businesses and organisations across Wales that would nurture and grow the foundations of the Welsh economy. Grants of up to £100,000 were offered for experiments that would be collaborative and innovative, challenging conventional ways of doing things and testing which interventions would work best. It was a way of seeking new directions for policy from local people, with £2.4m ring-fenced for projects within the Valleys. Since then, grants have been awarded to all geographical parts of Wales from Flintshire to Blaenau Gwent and to the social care sector. The

Foundational Economy will be promoted wherever possible with the positive outcomes of experiments spread across Wales. Social enterprises and small and medium-sized firms rooted in their communities will be supported to procure services and materials, creating local jobs. Local hospitals and schools will buy, wherever possible, locally produced food and PPE equipment.

Covid-19 emphasised the importance of the Foundational Economy. It was the local infrastructure of hospitals, care homes, postal deliveries and food shops that kept going during lockdowns. Wherever possible, expenditure that goes outside Wales should be replaced by local spending, retaining income in Wales and supporting local and regional economies. These ideas stand in the tradition of nineteenth and early-twentieth-century mutualism when local authorities and voluntary efforts provided in Wales clean water, schools, universities, houses, local swimming pools, hospitals, libraries, the Tredegar health scheme, and miners' institutes.

Places Matter

Ideas are easier to propose than to carry out. They demand new relationships and local ways of working. But where community wealth building has been tried, it has brought results. The often-quoted examples are Cleveland in the United States and Preston in Lancashire where in both cases traditional industries had collapsed. The adoption of community wealth building in Preston between 2013 and 2017 meant the amount spent in the local economy increased from £38m to £111m.

Unemployment was reduced below the UK average. There was a 10 per cent rise in those aged 16–24 receiving NVQ qualifications, and in 2018 Preston was named 'most improved city in the UK'. By 2020 it had achieved its highest employment rate for more than fifteen years. Wales is not Preston but the principles of community wealth building remain relevant.

An instructive example is the post-war housing estate at Lawrence Weston in north-west Bristol where poor transport links had left the estate cut off socially and economically. A local community group attracted a Lidl supermarket, supported a new bus service, improved recreational facilities, created a new community centre and developed a solar farm with the city council and a local energy co-operative. Profits are now invested in local projects and local employment has increased.

Covid-19 slowed local initiatives throughout Britain but it also emphasised the importance of community and place. The Welsh Government is pressing ahead in a variety of ways and localities with the self-help principles of local procurement and investment. But local councils are central to the process, dealing daily with local businesses. The spread and development of Foundational Economy ideas, uplifting towns and communities across Wales, ultimately depends upon the interest and involvement of local people and the commitment of local councils, their officers and elected members.

A remarkable variant exists in Blaenau Ffestiniog where a new economy is being developed based upon local social and community enterprise. Unlike the history of economic development in Wales which brought outside capital to develop the economy while the profits were spent elsewhere, in Blaenau Ffestiniog wealth is grown locally and retained for the community. It is a development which has lessons for many parts of Wales (Bevan Foundation, 12 January 2024).

13

Towards a New Economy

Il faut cultiver notre jardin
(We must cultivate our garden.)
Voltaire (*Candide*, 1759)

Britain, and particularly Wales, has a formidable agenda: learn the lessons of the pandemic, build a new economy, train people in the new skills required so that they can find work with decent pay, build homes for all and, by changing the way we live avoid, or at least mitigate, climate change. As the Covid-19 pandemic waned, the 'cost-of-living crisis', characterised by low productivity and sharply rising bills for food and energy, became the biggest squeeze on household incomes since records began in 1956–57. As the Covid-19 pandemic ends, the inherited problems of the Welsh economy remain.

The character of the last 200 years of industrialisation has been summed up by Rayworth (page ?) as Take, Make, Use, Lose. She pithily describes what has been a ubiquitous economic model and captures with accuracy the copper, iron, steel, tinplate and coal industries where raw materials were extracted from the earth, manufactured and after use discarded; a process that was repeated over and over in the nineteenth century as the

British economy developed. That system has no place in the future. The new British economy will not use materials once only. Single-use plastics have been banned in Wales since 30 October 2023. They were already banned in England and Scotland. New energy resources already in use will expand, there will be new industries and services, people will be trained for these new jobs, a range of 'green' measures will increase employment and mitigate the effects of global warming. Such an economy, the Circular Economy, keeps resources in use as long as possible by encouraging repair, recycling and re-use. Wales has one of the highest recycling rates in the world, third behind Germany and Taiwan. Twenty years ago Wales recycled less than 5 per cent of municipal waste, now it recycles more than 65 per cent. To achieve this, a billion pounds has been invested by the Welsh Government in waste collection and recycling. From April 2024 all businesses, charities and public sector organisations have been required by law to sort their waste for recycling. The ambition is to make Wales a zero-waste nation by 2050 with 100 per cent recycling, composting or preparing material for manufacturing. The raw materials retained in Wales will potentially create more jobs. A growing trend, partly caused by increased poverty, is the number of people who now recycle or re-use goods. In 2023 the National Survey for Wales found that 53 per cent of people were cutting down on buying brand-new items, compared to 46 per cent previously; the percentage of people in Wales who had either bought or been given second-hand items in the previous twelve months was 70 per cent compared with 57 per cent in 2018–19.

Town Centres

A major issue surrounds the future of the 192 places with populations over 2,000, the Welsh towns. They all face major challenges. Traditionally towns have been at the heart of Welsh life but the loss of industries has drained the life out of many of them, while the pandemic hastened changes to town centres and the way we use them. Out-of-town retailing has increased steadily since the 1980s and shopping online, already in use, accelerated during the pandemic. Increasingly the town centre is no longer the sole shopping area. Across Britain, approaching seventy retail companies have closed since January 2020, never to reopen. Between 2012 and 2020, 200 bank and building society branches in Welsh towns closed, a fall of more than a quarter. More have closed since.

The regeneration of town centres is therefore a priority of the Welsh Government. Between 2014 and 2021, it provided almost £900m to regenerate town centres by bringing empty buildings back into use and encouraging town centre working and learning. The 'Town Centres First' strategy put town centres at the heart of Welsh Government decisions on locating public offices and services. Modern office space and new homes are intended to provide attractive places for private investment and businesses. Small and middle-sized businesses continue to be firmly rooted in these local communities. In March 2022 a Welsh Government publication *Smarter Working: a remote working strategy for Wales* aimed to make Welsh towns hives of work and activity as once they were. Vacant buildings will be turned into flats or co-working hubs like the Welsh ICE project in Caerphilly. (Also at Caerphilly, work proceeds on a new market, the first project in the town's £20m regeneration scheme.)

The Welsh Government has estimated that around 30 per cent of workers in Wales could work regularly, or for two or three days a week, from home or in hubs providing working facilities within walking or cycling distance from home. This would reduce traffic congestion and carbon emissions and reduce spending in cafes in London or other city centres, while providing opportunities to contribute to communal life in their localities. Public-sector organisations will locate offices in town centres.

Lower spending in cafes and sandwich bars in London, Bristol, Newport, Cardiff and Swansea would be compensated by increased spending in local communities and the opportunity to contribute to communal life instead of spending hours commuting. Those most able to work from home or from local hubs are professional, administrative and clerical workers. Increasing numbers of workers could enjoy the local facilities of their home towns: eating out and using local and public services – post offices, libraries, council one-stop shops, repair cafes (with more than thirty, Wales has the largest network in the world), learning and community centres, art exhibitions, festivals of various kinds – and a variety of locally owned shops. High streets have changed, becoming centres of social interaction rather than places where one only went to do shopping.

New Energy Sources

Global warming means that we must halt, or at the very least mitigate, its effects. Coal, gas and petrol are being replaced by tidal and wind power, by hydrogen, and by nuclear energy. In 2020 half of the electricity used in Wales came from renewable sources. All buses in Wales will be hydrogen fuelled by 2028. By 2030 it is expected that carbon emissions will be cut by two-thirds compared with 1999 levels, with 70 per cent of electricity in Wales produced by wind, sun and tidal power. By 2050 Wales plans to be 'net zero' which means that the amount of greenhouse gases produced will be equalled by the amount removed from the atmosphere. With the sea on three sides there is the potential to harness the power of the tides and to go a long way to solving Wales' and the UK's energy problems, as well as creating thousands of jobs. The Welsh coastline has some of the best tidal energy possibilities in the world. The Morlais site on the west coast of Anglesey has the UK's largest agreed tidal energy scheme. The turbines involved will sit on the seabed and generate power as the tide comes in and as it goes out. The go-ahead has been given to a huge wind farm, the Awel Y Mor scheme, which will have fifty turbines off the coast of Llandudno. It is aiming to complete before 2030 with the maximum height of its turbines at 332 metres. The Crown Estate has plans to deliver 4GW of renewable energy by 2035 through developments in the Celtic Sea between Wales and Devon and Cornwall. New turbine technology using tidal energy is being investigated. On land more than three-quarters of the proposed wind farms had not been built in December 2023 while more than half had yet to enter the planning system. Many may not come to fruition. But hundreds, maybe thousands, of jobs will be created at sea along with a great expansion of renewable energy. The announcement that Wales will have two Free Ports has stimulated ideas for building at Port Talbot enormous floating wind turbines which would be located in the Celtic Sea. A multi-million pound bid to expand Pembroke Dock and enable it to become a key port for offshore wind farms has been submitted. Decisions have yet to be announced.

The Infrastructure (Wales) Bill, introduced to the Senedd in June 2023, gives Welsh ministers the power to consent to offshore and onshore generating stations, overhead electric lines, works to highways and railways and wastewater treatment plants. It introduces a simplified and effective consenting regime to the delivery of vital infrastructure projects. The eventual Act is expected to come into force in summer 2025. The stated preference of the Welsh Government is that 'where possible, new power lines should be laid underground'.

At Trawsfynydd, the former nuclear power station is likely to become a site for a mini nuclear plant. The Wylfa site on Anglesey is also expected to house a nuclear plant.

The Swansea Port Development Project envisages solar battery manufacture at Swansea docks, a solar farm creating one of the UK's largest solar energy facilities, a restaurant, a research centre and waterfront homes. The project is expected to provide up to 2,500 jobs and contribute £114m to the local economy. Work is expected to begin in 2025. Other ideas include a hydrogen pipeline from Pembroke to the Swansea Bay area connecting hydrogen production with industrial and domestic users, and an energy system at Felindre which would store excess electricity in batteries and then return it to the grid when demand increases.

More than a hundred years after first being proposed in 1920 the Severn Estuary, which has the second highest tidal range in the world, is once again being assessed as a source of energy. A tidal barrage across the Severn Estuary could supply around 7 per cent of the UK's energy needs. The Economic Advisory Council in April 1933 published a strongly favourable report. In the 1970s the idea was supported by the Wales TUC as a means of providing work for thousands. The idea was revived in 2008 but quashed following opposition from Avonmouth docks. In 2024 a cross-border body, the Western Gateway Partnership, a non-statutory body made up of local authorities, businesses and academics decided to once again investigate the idea.

While wind farms at sea have general approval, the numerous proposals for the erection of wind farms on Welsh land are hotly disputed. Pylons are seen as unnecessary blights on the scenic landscape destroying precious farming land, while some of the wind farms proposed are taller than the Blackpool Tower. Various campaign groups have argued that there needs to be an independent review into the up-to-date costs of placing power lines underground compared with the erection of pylons and the effects upon surrounding land. The Campaign for the Protection of Rural Wales has argued that onshore solar farms are threatening to 'industrialise' the Welsh countryside and ruin an unspoilt landscape.

UK Research and Innovation is investing £20m in the South Wales economy to reduce emissions and decarbonise industry. This would make it the first net zero emissions industrial area by 2040. Working towards that also is South Wales Industrial Cluster (SWIC) a partnership of South Wales businesses employing altogether more than 100,000 people, and Net Zero Industry Wales, a body created by the Welsh Government, which aims to ensure that industrial activities align to Welsh Government priorities.

Grow More Food

The greatest and most important future change could be a new range of foods produced by little more than thin air. On Anglesey, experiments funded by the Welsh Government and undertaken by a partnership of Menter Môn and the Lafan Consulting Group are currently producing a variety of food products by fermenting hydrogen using bacteria. The foods contain proteins which are said to be 'healthy and tasty'. These experiments, if successful, could transform the future of the planet. While we await the outcome of these experiments, much is already happening. It was Covid-19 that made us realise that the food on our plates, usually taken for granted, was at the mercy of fluctuations in the global market. Empty supermarket shelves demonstrated that Wales imports half its vegetables and more than 80 per cent of its fruit. It suddenly seemed common sense to produce locally as much as possible to safeguard supplies. And that raised the issue of 'food miles'. The distance from grower to consumer, from farm to fork, indicates the extent of environmental damage caused by the emission of carbon dioxide from aeroplanes, ships and lorries. The environmental crisis has consequences for the food we eat, the houses we live in, the transport we use, the jobs that need doing, and much else.

Growing food locally in gardens, allotments and farms reduces the carbon footprint caused by importing food and increases local supplies of food. In short, whenever possible eat locally produced food and support local shops and markets. The organisations Bannau Acres and Bannau Brycheiniog have a network of independent farms growing fruit and vegetables in Powys, Monmouthshire and Breconshire. Those parts of the food industry in Wales that depend upon public contracts with colleges, schools, local government and hospitals are essential producers. Monmouthshire County Council aims to supply all its primary schools with locally grown fruit and vegetables. Across Wales at four locations – Cwmbran, Treorchy, Wrexham and Newtown – an experiment, funded by the Welsh Government and using science and technology to perfect plant production, is producing food bought and consumed locally. This experiment both increases local food supplies and increases the number of local jobs, while better food reduces calls upon the NHS. Other schemes with great promise are the growing of food vertically and growing food by the use of hydroponics. The advantages of hydroponics are that plants can be grown anywhere the whole year round without the need for heating or ventilation. The aim will be to develop local food supply chains across the country. Thousands of jobs could come from green developments in agriculture, land and forestry. But those food experiments on Anglesey and elsewhere in Britain, if successful, would be world-changing.

Houses and Transport

Too many people in Britain are homeless, a fact which would have shocked both Aneurin Bevan and Harold Macmillan. In October 2023 in Wales there were 139,000 people, including 3,409 children, on social housing waiting lists; 11,200, including 3,409 children, were in temporary accommodation; and around 135 people were sleeping on the streets (Chartered Institute of Housing Cymru). These numbers are increasing. The Chartered Institute of Housing Cymru, Shelter Cymru and *Tai Pawb* all argue that everyone should have the legal right to adequate housing, a view supported by over 70 per cent of people in Wales. Research by Alma Economics using HM Treasury guidelines compared the right to adequate housing with the benefits it would bring over a thirty-year period. The research suggests that providing adequate housing would generate £11.5bn worth of benefits while costing £5bn.

Of course house building in a variety of ways is taking place all over Wales. Many owner-occupiers have fitted solar panels to their houses. The Pobl Group, the largest housing association in Wales, aims to build 10,000 energy-efficient houses across Wales by 2030. In North Wales Cartrefi Conwy, a not-for-profit social landlord, is building new affordable zero-carbon social homes. The Swansea Bay City Deal has an initiative – 'Homes as power stations' – which has received approval from the UK and Welsh governments. The project envisages the construction of 3,300 houses and the fitting of 7,000 others with green technology, such as solar panels, heat pumps and batteries instead of gas boilers. A pilot project on six bungalows at Craigcefnparc in the Swansea valley resulted in energy bills for residents falling from an average of £71 in January 2020 to £3 for the first three weeks in April 2020.

The Welsh Government is working with eleven local authorities to deliver a system of net zero carbon timber-framed houses. For this purpose, wood is environmentally superior to bricks, cement or plastic and the wood can be grown in Wales. The Construction Industry Training Board estimates that 12,000 new jobs will be created in Wales by building green homes and retrofitting others. Training in the new skills is now a priority. Green homes kill four birds with one stone: more modern homes, more jobs, fewer people in fuel poverty, and a response to the climate emergency.

The 2021 Census revealed that the M4 corridor is attracting thousands of new houses with most building taking place in the Cardiff and Newport areas. Newly built homes eradicate fuel poverty; building them creates thousands of jobs. But the most urgent need is for houses for the more than 100,000 in Wales without permanent homes. A statutory registration and licensing scheme for all visitor accommodation in Wales will be introduced to the Senedd before the end of 2024. Across the UK too the need is great. Lloyds Bank and the charity Crisis are calling for one million new, genuinely affordable homes to be built by 2033. Building homes for all in need should be a priority of the next government.

Transport is an area where huge changes are taking place. The switch to electric cars by private car owners is under way. Electric charging points are being posted every twenty miles on major routes. Electric buses are being introduced in a number of Welsh local authorities including Gwynedd, refuse lorries are being electrified. The scheme to introduce electric trains was described in Chapter 9. A new road linking North and South Wales was opened in February 2024. Built near Machynlleth, and crossing the River Dyfi it links with the A487 and replaces a nineteenth-century bridge that is frequently flooded.

New Jobs

Manufacturing remains a significant part of the Welsh economy with 150,000 people directly employed in that sector and thousands more employed in supply chains. It contributes 16 per cent to Welsh national output, whereas the UK contribution of manufacturing to the national output is around 9 per cent. Decarbonising this sector in Wales, developing the necessary workforce skills, and providing resilient supply chains are among the priorities identified by the Welsh Government.

Most of the top-fifty firms in Wales are sited in Newport, Cardiff, Swansea, Wrexham and on Deeside. The Cardiff/Newport area, including the aerospace-centred Bro Tathan business park in the Vale of Glamorgan, is the favoured location for the fast-growing new industries of the future providing well-paid jobs focused around compound semi-conductor technology, smart phones, Wi-Fi, satellite communication systems, cyber security, artificial intelligence, robotics, and bio-engineering. Newport has a thriving semi-conductor cluster including the US firm Vishay Intertechnology which is investing £1bn in the Nexperia plant acquired for £144m from its Chinese owners. Microsoft is investing in the Cardiff/Newport area creating around 120 jobs in the development of artificial intelligence. Rolls-Royce has confirmed that a planned business park on the outskirts of Cardiff could be the site for almost 200 highly skilled jobs. In addition Rolls-Royce has confirmed that the proposed Cardiff Parkway rail station could be at the heart of a new business district and the site for considerable expansion by Rolls-Royce. In Cardiff the professional services firm PwC is creating 1,000 jobs. Panasonic is investing up to £20m in Cardiff to develop a centre of excellence for Green Technologies within the UK. Along the M4 corridor the broadband firm Ogi is introducing a high-speed fibre network. When completed it will move millions of gigabits along the corridor, boosting the Welsh economy and bringing highly skilled jobs to the region. At Bridgend 200 permanent jobs are expected as developer Robert Hitchens expands on the industrial estate.

A £50m fund was unveiled in October 2022 aimed at tripling productivity growth in the Welsh media landscape across Wales in the next five years. In 2023 the US Great Point Studios acquired Cardiff film studios from the Welsh Government with the aim of expanding film and TV production and media training. In North Wales a new television and film studio has opened in Llangefni, Anglesey, supported by S4C and the Welsh Government.

The giant Airbus firm, the largest civil airspace company in the UK which in 2023 employed 5,500 at its wing-making factory at Broughton and 500 people at Newport, intends to create a further 1,100 jobs. Many of these will be in Wales. Airbus is also the biggest space satellite company in the UK where there are ambitious plans for space exploration, involving Wales as well as England and Scotland. Already there are 160 companies in Wales employing more than 2,300 people in the aerospace industry. Swansea University's Department of Aerospace Engineering introduces students to space flight simulators. The UK Space Agency is supporting a Cardiff aerospace company, Small Spark Space Systems, that is developing new rocket propulsion systems. The Space

Forge company in Cardiff is pioneering returnable space satellites designed to manufacture products in space that will be purer than those manufactured on Earth. Potentially these will include chemicals, vaccines, alloys and microelectronics. The first exploratory Welsh satellite launch from Cornwall in January 2023 ended in failure but further launches will follow. Space Forge has also received £7.9m to build a National Microgravity Research Centre, the first of its kind in Europe. In North Wales, Snowdonia LLP has received £800,000 to develop a Space Technology Test Centre. The Welsh Government is determined that Wales will be at the forefront of the space industry. Meanwhile Cawdor Barracks, near St David's in Pembrokeshire has been identified by the Ministry of Defence as the UK's preferred site for a new radar system which will detect, track and identify objects in deep space. Around 100 permanent jobs will be provided.

The most important immediate boost to the Welsh economy will be the two Free Ports, one at Holyhead and the other covering Milford Haven and Port Talbot. They are expected to begin operations by the end of 2023. Each will benefit from simplified customs procedures, relief on customs duties, and tax benefits, while each will receive £26m of seed funding from the UK Government. Potentially they could create 20,000 new jobs with many more in prospect. At the insistence of the Welsh Government, the Free Ports will promote fair work opportunities and prioritise environmental sustainability.

In addition to the Airbus developments at Broughton

already mentioned, there is considerable potential for job growth in North Wales. The UK Government has announced that more than 300 civil service jobs in the Department for Work and Pensions, and the Ministry of Justice will be moved to Wrexham, bringing an estimated economic benefit of around £9m to the area. The Deeside and Wrexham industrial estates make up the largest engineering and manufacturing hub in Europe with 34 per cent of the workforce involved in manufacturing. This includes the Indian-owned Ipsen life sciences firm which exports to more than 90 countries and is increasing its North Wales labour force. At Wrexham the university is developing its £30m Enterprise, Engineering and Optics Centre. M-Sparc, the science park owned by Bangor University, and AMRC, which is a £20m research centre managed by the University of Sheffield, have agreed to collaborate to secure joint funding. They will work together on knowledge sharing, engineering, agriculture, and advanced manufacturing. At Aberporth Europe's unmanned aerial systems firm, Tekever, will create around 100 highly skilled jobs over the next three years while Harlech Foodservice with headquarters near Criccieth will create 150 jobs over the same period. At Blaenau Ffestiniog local people with financial assistance from the Welsh Government have set up co-operatives and social enterprises, emphasising the importance of community self-help. In Llanberis the life science division of the Siemens Group, Siemens Healthcare, is creating 92 jobs in addition to the 400 already there. A range of new projects funded by the North Wales Growth Deal include an all-year Zip World cable car project, the development of science parks on Anglesey and elsewhere, and the Free Port at Holyhead with motorway access to Liverpool and Manchester and their airports. At Theatr Clwyd a £45m update will create 60 new jobs and it will be the first carbon-positive theatre in the UK. On the Wrexham Industrial Estate approval has been given for a 150,000 sq. ft industrial expansion for the developer FI Real Estate Management (FIREM). It is expected to support around 250 new jobs. FIREM also has plans for warehouse and office space which, when completed, could provide 1,200 jobs. A further sign of the economic vitality growing in North Wales is the application for an £80m Investment Zone in Wrexham and Flintshire made to the Welsh and British governments by a new consortium which includes the North Wales Business Council, Wrexham and Flintshire councils, Wrexham University and the Advanced Manufacturing Research Centre in Broughton.

To encourage more home-grown businesses, the Welsh Government has set up a £5m fund available over the years 2022 to 2025 for young people with the desire to start new businesses. Those with viable ideas will receive up to £2,000 per business, plus advisory support and mentoring, including business planning and help with financial management.

City Deals

City Deals, introduced by the Westminster Government in 2013, give a city and its surrounding areas powers to create economic growth and take responsibility for decisions that affect their area. The two in Wales, based on Cardiff and Swansea, are funded by both the UK and Welsh governments. In mid-Wales and North Wales there are Growth Deals which, although not based on cities, work on a variety of projects with the local authorities, businesses, hospitals and universities within their boundaries.

The £1.2bn Cardiff Capital City Region dating from 2016 is an agreement between the UK Government, the Welsh Government and the following ten local councils: Blaenau Gwent, Bridgend, Caerphilly, Cardiff, Merthyr Tydfil, Monmouthshire, Newport, Rhondda Cynon Taf, Torfaen and the Vale of Glamorgan. Some £734m of the £1.2bn is funding the Metro. The Swansea Bay City Region set up in 2017 is a partnership between the UK Government, the Welsh Government, and the local authorities of Swansea, Carmarthenshire, Neath Port Talbot and Pembrokeshire. These two City Deals are largely coterminous with the South Wales east and west regions.

The strategic plan for the Cardiff Capital City region over its twenty-year life cycle is to create 20,000 new jobs including 10,000 new apprenticeships, attract £4bn private sector investment and raise Gross Value Added (GVA) by 5 per cent. The redevelopment of a 30-acre site at Atlantic Wharf in Cardiff's Bute Town envisages new homes and offices, shops, hotel, restaurant and leisure projects. A £45m fund supports the building of 2,800 new homes across the city region. The region also takes

143

responsibility for the regional Skills Partnership. While the task of the Skills Partnership is to raise the level of skills within the region as a whole the level of skills in the Valleys is a particular problem. In Cardiff 46 per cent of working-age people have qualifications at level 4 or above. In Caerphilly, Blaenau Gwent and Merthyr Tydfil the proportion is less than 33 per cent. Merthyr Tydfil in 2017 had the highest level of persons with absolutely no qualifications, 16.4 per cent. Right across the region there is a shortage of people with skills in digital technology. A £50m equity fund is available to invest in firms in the region. In addition, a fund of £9.5m will train more than 1,000 cyber-skilled individuals and increase the number of cyber security firms in the area.

The Swansea Bay City Region, with a £1.3bn fund, has a fifteen-year time span from 2017. Its aims include generating 9,000 jobs through nine ambitious projects. These include concentrating upon skills and training for around 17,000 people, digital connections right across the area, encouragement of the creative industries, including a Swansea Arena, an entertainment centre, a new waterfront district and events to create an all-season visitor destination. Regeneration of the Lower Swansea Valley includes a new Penderyn whisky distillery and visitor centre. At Pembroke Dock marine energy developments will reduce the cost of energy; at Llanelli there will be a life science and health centre called Pentre Awel. The 'Homes as Power Stations' project which has been approved by the UK and Welsh governments will build 3,300 new houses and retrofit another 7,000 thereby reducing carbon emissions and saving domestic energy bills.

The original aim of creating 9,000 jobs has been set back by the projected loss of around 2,000 jobs at the Port Talbot steelworks where the owners, Tata Steel, who are losing £1m a day at Port Talbot, announced in January 2024 that it would close the blast furnaces and move to low-carbon steel production. The steelworks has been one of the UK's largest polluters. A £1.2bn package has been agreed between the UK Government and Tata Steel to help those made redundant, estimated to be around 2,000 in England and Wales with the bulk, 1,929, at Port Talbot. The UK Government will provide £500m with the remaining funding coming from Tata. The deal will enable the current blast furnace steelworks to become an electric arc furnace operation. A Transition Board has been set up with access to the £100m which will be used to invest in skills and regenerate the Neath Port Talbot economy. The changes at Port Talbot mean that the UK will be the world's only major economy unable to make primary steel from raw materials, making it dependent upon imported primary steel. Trade unions are strongly objecting to this outcome and hope that if there is a Labour government in the near future, a different development may be possible.

Training and Education

None of the new jobs will be possible without people with the skills to carry them out. The 2021 Census revealed that almost one-fifth of the Welsh labour force lacked any recognised qualifications. More recent studies suggest that one out of two new jobs will require new skills due to automation and digitalisation while the increasing use of artificial intelligence is expected to increase the demand for graduates. There are fears too that there will not be sufficient craftsmen to replace those who retire. There is a particular concern over a shortage of skilled workers in small to medium enterprises. The need in general in the UK is for joiners, welders, heat pump engineers, electrical engineers, technicians and construction workers. A huge effort to upskill the Welsh labour force is therefore required. The Welsh Government in February 2022 announced that it would invest £366m in apprenticeship training over the next three years with the intention of recruiting 125,000 apprentices by 2026. Changes to the draft budget have reduced this number to 115,000, despite protests by employers' organisations. A valuable possible development is the creation of a National Technological Institute at Newport, providing around 3,000 students with the technical skills essential to current and future developments. Newport Council has applied to the Westminster Government's levelling up fund for support.

14

Future Wales

What's past is prologue
Shakespeare (*The Tempest*, act 2, sc. 1)

The 1851 Census revealed that Wales was probably the first country in the world to have more people employed in industry and services than in agriculture. It was a narrow range of industries – copper, iron and steel, coal and slate – upon which to build an industrial economy. After 1945 modern factories and new service employments flourished for some forty years. And now, after fifty years of deindustrialisation followed by Brexit and Covid-19, the task of creating a new Wales has finally begun. The next ten years will be crucial to the future of planet Earth. It is then that worldwide essential actions to deal with climate change must be taken. The constitutional future of Wales and the United Kingdom could be decided in that time too. There are real fears that the environmental problems of planet Earth may not be solved. June 2023 was the hottest June on record, globally and for the UK. But if the environmental problems were solved, what might the new Wales look like?

A New Wales

The constitutional question is the most uncertain. It depends in large part upon the actions taken by Scotland and Northern Ireland and by governments in Westminster. The people of Northern Ireland voted to remain in the European Union. However, Sinn Fein which stands for a united Ireland is now in the majority in the Northern Ireland Assembly. If Sinn Fein continues in strength and Northern Ireland were to become part of the Republic, it would automatically become part of the European Union. A united Ireland remains possible.

If, in the next twenty years the flame of Scottish independence revives and Scotland were to leave the UK and join the EU, what of Wales? Control by Westminster runs counter to political developments in Wales and, according to a report in October 2023 by the Institute for Public Policy Research (IPPR), such 'muscular unionism' by Westminster is not in tune with UK popular feeling. A federal UK may be one answer but it is not currently being proposed by either Tory or Labour Westminster governments. Could Wales break away and be an independent nation within a federal Europe? That would mean an end to 'the United Kingdom'. It is unlikely though not impossible as Will Hayward has discussed in *Independent Nation*. The next ten years will make these issues clearer.

Population

In the new Wales the population could be substantially increased by immigrants fleeing climate change as millions move from tropical regions to cooler zones. Consequently the population will be younger, a change already noticed in the 2021 Census where population growth in Wales was driven by immigrants, 94 per cent of whom were aged under 45 years. The native Welsh population is ageing. By 2038 almost 20 per cent of the native population will be aged 70 and over. The trend for Welsh people who have worked elsewhere but upon retirement have decided to return to Wales will almost certainly continue. A National Care Service for the elderly will be in place, replacing what was described by the NHS Confederation in September 2022 as being in a state of 'national emergency'. The drift from the Valleys will have continued with populations growing in Newport, Cardiff, Swansea and Wrexham. New homes will be built in these cities. Children will be healthier. Welsh speakers may have increased but will remain a minority. The growth of second homes in Wales, often left empty in the winter, will have ceased. There will be a right, enshrined in law, for local residents to have a home.

Flora and fauna will be protected and thrive. The planting of underwater grass meadows absorbing carbon dioxide and helping to attract marine wildlife will be widespread around Welsh coasts. Peat will not be allowed in compost and there will be wide-scale restoration of peatlands, preventing the release of 20 million tonnes of carbon dioxide each year. Single-use plastic will have long disappeared.

The current experiments with producing food using hydrogen are hugely important. If successful, they could change the future of the planet. Even if not eventually successful, much more of the food on our plates will be grown in England and Wales with large-scale industrial greenhouses an important source. The more than thirty vineyards currently in Wales will have increased and be flourishing in the higher temperatures. A higher proportion of the labour force than the current 4 per cent will be employed in horticulture and agriculture.

Energy Sources

Energy supplies will come from sea, wind and sun power. Probably also from nuclear power stations in North Wales. Tidal power will be harnessed by a variety of schemes. There will be wind farms sited in the Celtic Sea bordering the west and north of Wales. Wind farms on land, particularly in the South Wales Valleys, will have increased to meet demand but will then decline as offshore wind farms increase. Wales will be a net exporter of energy. A possible source will be geothermal heating coming from the abandoned deep coal mines. In 2021 the former Cornish tin mines were already providing this energy locally. A Welsh Clean Air Act will have been in place for many years. Gas boilers will not exist. Diesel and petrol cars, lorries and buses will have been long replaced by electric vehicles with charging points available every twenty miles on major routes. Congestion charges for car users will be in operation in Cardiff and Swansea, probably in Newport and Wrexham too. They already are in place in London and Birmingham. The 20 mph speed limit in built-up areas has been enforced since

September 2023. There will be net zero greenhouse gas emissions. A National Forest will be growing from North to South Wales. The Clwydian Range and Dee Valley will be a National Park. The Cambrian Mountains in mid-Wales will be designated an Area of Outstanding Natural Beauty if not a National Park.

Homes will be energy efficient. Thousands of new low-carbon homes to buy or rent will have been built resulting in zero or low-energy bills. Many will provide electric car charging points. All new school, college and hospital buildings and refurbishments will be carbon neutral. The use of Welsh wood as a building material will be well established. Around a third of the labour force, including many entrepreneurs, will work from their homes or local 'hubs', anchoring them in their communities instead of spending hours commuting.

It will be a Wales where, away from the cities, the emphasis will be upon 'place'. Locally led initiatives will utilise the assets and strengths of local communities. Local authorities with Banc Cambria will play an important role in fostering their local economies. Industrial and housing developments on 'greenfield' sites will not be allowed, taking place only in existing industrial locations and towns. The high-profile manufacturing and service employments of the future will continue to be based primarily near or on the coasts in Wrexham and Deeside and on the southern industrial sites close to the M4. The major aerospace and insurance companies will still be important employers. But new industries and services as yet unthought of will have developed out of the life sciences and tech industries that will be generating new jobs. A new medical school will be long-established at Bangor. Also in north-west Wales will be a public sector National Laboratory with its own nuclear reactor. It will be producing medical radioisotopes and supplying them to the Wales NHS and other NHS services in England, Scotland and Ireland for the diagnosis and treatment of cancers. In Carmarthenshire a new multi-million-pound hospital will be in service at Whitland or St Clears.

Developments on coastal locations will include the Pembroke Dock Marine technology project, the £100m redevelopment of Holyhead waterfront, the Lanza Tech factory in Port Talbot converting the gases produced by the making of steel at Port Talbot into sustainable aviation fuel. The floating homes in Atlantic Wharf, Cardiff and the £1.7bn 'Blue Eden' project at Swansea Bay will provide homes, battery manufacturing and storage, a solar farm and a climate change research centre.

The Welsh labour force will contain both robots and highly skilled workers. At least 90 per cent of those aged 16–24 will be in education, training or employment. Working-age adults will be much better qualified, 75 per cent will have level 3 qualifications or higher, many with green skills. The pay gap resulting from gender, ethnicity or disability will have been seriously reduced if not eliminated. The four-day working week will be normal. Private firms and public bodies will buy goods and products recycled or using low-carbon materials like wood. Repair cafes and re-use facilities will be sited in town centres. Schoolchildren will be educated in the significance of climate change, energy use and the importance of recycling and re-use. There will be investment in green skills with appropriate apprenticeships, training and reskilling for current and future jobs.

Away from the main industrial locations and the cities of Cardiff, Swansea, Newport and Wrexham, Wales will be a country of natural scenery and thriving towns where a combination of green projects, vertical farming, Foundational Economics and the Circular Economy, will produce strong local businesses. There will be good communications by rail and bus. Sixty per cent of Welsh workers will be employed in small and medium-sized firms spread throughout Wales where fair work practices will be the legal norm. Every town will have green spaces. The Valley towns will be greener and cleaner. People will be healthier and fitter, the Valleys' Park and local woodlands providing healthy surroundings in addition to the adjacent open mountainsides. Valley towns will be connected to each other by cycle routes through former rail tunnels, by the A465, by electric buses and to the coast by the Metro. There will be integrated rail connections to North and South Wales. Car ownership will have fallen with many people making use of buses, trains, or a local pool of cars (car clubs) for their journeys. High-speed email digital connections will be available to all households, enabling links with friends and family, access to sources of information and education and the opportunity to shop and work from home. Merthyr Tydfil, Ebbw Vale, Pontypridd, Caerphilly and Bridgend will be important employment centres for the Valleys.

Cultural Centres

Tourism will continue to be a major source of jobs and income throughout Wales with public and private money going into hotels, coastal and heritage sites, outdoor activities, the National Parks, the National Botanic Garden of Wales, and the National Museum in Cardiff. The Welsh name for the Brecon Beacons National Park – Bannau Brycheiniog – will be in popular use. The medieval castles at Caerphilly, Harlech, Caernarfon, Conwy, Beaumaris, the Blaenafon industrial landscape, the Cyfarthfa site, Gwynedd slate district, and Pontcysyllte Aqueduct, will be major attractions. There will be a National Gallery of Contemporary Art in addition to a variety of museums and art galleries throughout Wales which showcase Welsh artists. Musicians, painters and sculptors, actors and writers are part of Wales' history and heritage but also part of the present and future. In September 2022 the Welsh Government announced a £1m fund to develop talent in the music, digital content and film and TV industries. Theatres, film and TV studios will in future be busy providing work for international and Welsh talent despite the 2024 difficulties of National Theatre Wales.

Universities, through their research centres and teaching, will play a full part in developing the new Wales. The further education colleges will be providing the skills and training essential for caring, cooking, tourism, farming and land management, and the new tech industries. A more equal society will be investing in people and their potential, providing lifelong learning opportunities for individuals to develop and grow emotionally and intellectually. It will be a Wales with a sense of well-being and purpose.

Necessary Steps

This is an optimistic vision of a future Wales. Will it happen and can we afford it? Why would we not? What matters to individuals is well known: their health, employment, homes, food, fair pay and leisure. As citizens we all need security, medical care, quality education, and a friendly environment. Let us will the means to achieve these for all and not just for a privileged minority. We know now that poverty does not disappear as the economy grows. Instead, relative poverty increases and actual poverty does not disappear unless dealt with positively. Taxation is the means by which we collectively find the funds to do what needs to be done. These are issues to be determined by future governments but three aspects cry out for change.

Income from wealth is under-taxed compared with taxes upon wages, salaries and pensions. Therefore, tax accumulated wealth. The International Monetary Fund, in April 2021, called for increased taxation on wealth to help fund recovery from the pandemic. Individuals and small and medium-sized companies are paying more than their fair share through various taxes, while wealthy individuals and global multinational companies, through deliberate policies, are paying very much less than their fair share. An analysis by Oxfam in 2023 revealed that in the UK the combined wealth of the richest 1 per cent is equivalent to the wealth of 70 per cent of the population. The pandemic was a time of fear and sorrow for millions. It was also a time of enormous profit for Google, Apple, Microsoft, Tesla, Facebook and Amazon and the fortunes of their leading figures. With those fortunes comes political power, and the economic power to dominate markets by buying out aspiring competitors. The ambitions of these controlling individuals and corporations threaten democracy.

There should be a land value tax. Decisions on land use made by planners and local councils can produce huge windfall gains for landowners. Some of that gain should be reclaimed for public purposes. The tax has the advantage of being relatively hard to avoid and is one supported by both the left and the right (the right on the grounds, said Milton Friedman, that it would be the least bad tax). Wales does not presently have these tax-raising powers but the United Kingdom has them and should use them. By 2050 they will surely be used. There is too the issue of council tax. The previous revaluation in Wales was in 2003. There will be another before 2026 and, probably, at least another after that.

15

The Unanswered Question

If we are to live well, within the limits of a finite
planet, we need a better conception of social progress
than the one encoded in the myth of growth.
Tim Jackson (*Post Growth*, 2021)

Economic growth is not a myth. It is real and we are
addicted to it. It is often beneficial as Jackson concedes,
yet its unthinking pursuit obscures gross inequalities
while its unchecked consequences are a threat to the
survival of planet Earth. Despite improvements in our
material circumstances, we have always wanted more.
Jackson quotes the Chinese philosopher, Lao Tzu, who
two and a half thousand years ago said:

That enough's enough
Is enough to know.

In Britain since the fourteenth century there has been
a common saying: 'Enough is as good as a feast.' Yet we
do not know how to switch off that urge for more. Over
a century ago in his 1905 book *Socialism and Society*,
Ramsay MacDonald wrote on page one: 'Poverty still
challenges the reason and conscience of men, and instead

of becoming less acute as national wealth increases, it becomes more serious.' Relentlessly under the influence of mass advertising, the appeal to greed continues to corrode our better instincts. Believing that more of everything is the source of happiness, it took the pandemic, a time of fear and sorrow, to remind us of Ruskin's conclusion: 'There is no wealth but life.'

Statistics of economic growth hide the realities of our economic system. The liberal concept of inevitable progress and ever-increasing wealth, born in the industrialisation of the nineteenth century, is now under increasing scrutiny in the Western world from a variety of economists and commentators: Schumacher (1974), Hirsch (1976), Hutton (1996), Hertz (2001), Kingsnorth (2008), Wilkinson and Pickett (2009), Skidelski (2013), Lansley and Mack (2015), Sayer (2015), McGarvey (2017), Rayworth (2017), and Jackson (2021). More than sixty years ago, J. K. Galbraith's *Affluent Society* (1958) powerfully analysed the 'conventional wisdom', demonstrating how private affluence and public squalor grow side by side. After initial acclaim, it was largely forgotten. Thirty-six years later in St David's Hall, Cardiff, on 26 January 1994, Galbraith sketched out a vision of what the good society might be, building on his original analysis to include the effect of 'growth' upon individuals. Here is the heart of what he said:

Everyone should have a basic source of income. If not available from the market system, it must come from the state. Most important is human investment through education, and that also is a responsibility of the state.

So too is the provision of good low-cost housing, if the market does not provide it. And so too is health care. There must be state investment in the longer-run interest of the environment. A more equitable distribution of income is necessary and that will ensure a steadier flow of purchasing power in recessions. And in times of recession, governments must act to employ people, to mitigate distress. 'The good society does not allow some of its people to feel useless, superfluous and deprived.'

These were the basic needs that Galbraith chose to spell out in 1994. In Britain thirty years later not only do many people exist without them, but poverty – relative, and some cases actual – has grown. Galbraith's summary recalls Aneurin Bevan's comment: 'There is no test for progress other than its impact on the individual' (*In Place of Fear*, p. 200).

Growth with Well-being?

Throughout Britain, in affluent London as well as the former coal-mining areas, there is disabling poverty. The 'cost-of-living crisis' came to a society already deeply fractured with too many on low pay, too many without a home, and too many in jobs with low productivity. Real wages in 2022 were no higher than in 2008. Inflation in 2022 reached its highest level for forty years. Over six million people in 2023 were in fuel poverty. The Carnegie UK Trust has developed an alternative measure of social progress: Gross Domestic Wellbeing (GDWe). It takes into account social, environmental and domestic factors as well as economic. It is a promising development that puts statistical flesh upon the bones of the Well-being of Future Generations Act. So far it has only analysed the situation in England where collective well-being was found to be in decline well before the Covid-19 pandemic. This is not a surprise. One way not to achieve a better life is to cut back the everyday economy: health, care, education, and the budgets of local authorities. That mistake has dominated society ever since.

Today in Wales there is hopefully a growing understanding of our urgent responsibility to leave a better world to our grandchildren. That better world is possible but it will not be found in the unthinking pursuit of never-ending growth or in the exciting diversions of space travel. Exploration of space will continue but visions of the colonisation of Mars and the Moon are an escape from the realities of life on Earth, not a solution. Covid-19 showed that in crisis we have not forgotten the value of home and social stability, the bonds of community, and obligation to others. But 'normal' life – a return to constant growth without ameliorating its consequences – is not only a way of avoiding making a decision about existing inequalities, which, in turn, are increased by 'growth'. It is a threat to life on this planet.

There are two obvious tasks. Urgently over the next ten years we have to change the way we live in order to protect life on this planet. And we have to ensure that existing basic needs are met. People doing essential jobs should receive decent pay, everyone should have a home, and no one should have to choose between eating and heating. Relative poverty, and in too many cases actual poverty, has grown side by side with riches. If we will not tackle existing basic needs now, when will we? Food banks should not be a permanent feature of a country as rich as Britain. Our choice and task should not be in doubt. Listen to what people need and then work with them to deliver it, providing in towns, villages and cities, an economy and society that serves all the people. Is that so unreasonable?

AUTHOR

Joe England was educated at Cyfarthfa Grammar School, Merthyr Tydfil and at the University of Nottingham where he studied Economic and Social History. In a varied career he has been editor of a weekly newspaper, a full-time lecturer for the Workers Educational Association, Deputy Director of the Department of Extra-Mural Studies in the University of Hong Kong, Research Fellow in the Industrial Relations Research Unit at Warwick University, and Principal and Chief Executive of Coleg Harlech, Wales' residential college for adults. He has travelled widely in East Asia and is well known as a lecturer on social and industrial affairs. He has published a number of books including the critically acclaimed biography of place, *Merthyr: The Crucible of Modern Wales*.

ACKNOWLEDGEMENTS

I am grateful to Jeremy Gass, Geraint Talfan Davies, Dawn Bowden and Phil Bowyer for comments on an earlier draft. Judy Evans rescued the text when I thought I had lost it. Special thanks go to Dai Smith as Series Editor who, as ever, gave the text meticulous attention and made valuable suggestions.

REFERENCES

Alston, Philip. *Statement on Visit to the United Kingdom*, 16 November 2018.

Audit Wales, *Regenerating Town Centres in Wales*. September 2021.

Ballard, Paul H. and Jones, Erastus. *The Valleys Call* (Ron Jones Publications, Ferndale, 1975).

Beddoe, Deidre. *Out of the Shadows: A History of Women in Twentieth-Century Wales* (University of Wales Press, 2000).

Bevan, Aneurin. *In Place of Fear* (EP Publishing Limited, 1976) pp. 5, 113.

Calafati, L., et al. *When Nothing Works* (Manchester University Press, 2023).

Cooke, Phil. *Dependent Development in United Kingdom Regions with Particular Reference to Wales* (Progress in Planning, Vol. 15 Part One. p. 35).

Cunningham, Helen. *Anchor Towns*. Bevan Foundation, 2020.

Curtis, Ben. *The South Wales Miners' Federation and the perception and representation of risk and danger in the coal industry 1898–1947* (Morgannwg, The Journal of Glamorgan History, 2014) pp. 71–88.

England, Joe. *The Wales TUC 1974–2004* (University of Wales Press, 2004).

Foden, Fothergill, Gore. *The state of the coalfields: economic and social conditions in the former mining communities of*

REFERENCES

England, Scotland and Wales (Sheffield Hallam University Centre for Regional Economic and Social Research, 2014).

Francis, Hywel and Smith, David. *The Fed: a History of the South Wales Miners in the Twentieth Century* (Lawrence and Wishart, 1980).

Galbraith, Kenneth. *The Affluent Society* (Pelican Books, 1962).

Galbraith, J. K. *The Good Society Considered: the economic dimension* (St David's Hall, Cardiff, 26 January 1994. Journal of Law and Society, Cardiff Law School).

George and Mainwaring. *The Welsh Economy* (University of Wales Press, 1988) p. 14.

Griffiths, James. *Pages from Memory* (J. M. Dent, 1969).

Hertz, Noreena. *The Silent Takeover* (Arrow Books, 2002).

Hirsch, Fred. *Social Limits to Growth* (Harvard University Press, 1976).

Hopkins, Tony (ed,) *Blaenau Gwent Voices* (The Scrivenors, 2018).

Hutton, Will. *The State We're In* (Vintage Books, 1996).

Jack, Ian. *Before the Oil Ran Out: Britain 1977–1987* (Fontana, 1988) p. 83.

Jackson, Tim. *Post Growth* (Polity, 2021) p. 65.

Johnes, Martin. *Wales: England's Colony?* (Parthian, 2019).

Johnes, Martin. *Wales Since 1939* (Manchester University Press, 2012), p. 135.

Judt, Tony. *Ill Fares The Land* (Penguin Books, 2011).

Kingsnorth, Paul. *Real England* (Portobelo Books, 2009).

Leeworthy, Daryl. *Labour Country: Political Radicalism and Social Democracy in South Wales 1831–1985* (Parthian, 2018), pp. 267–8.

MacDonald, J. Ramsay. *Socialism and Society* (ILP, 1905) p. 1.

Marmot Review, *Health Equity in England: The Marmot Review 10 Years On* (Institute of Health Equity, February 2020).

McGarvey, Darren. *Poverty Safari* (Picador, 2017).

Morgan, Kevin. *Enhancing Institutional Capacity: Multi-level governance and territorial development in Wales* (Final Report to the OECD, December 2019).

PEP. *Location of Industry* (Political and Economic Planning, 1939).

Rayworth, Kate. *Doughnut Economics* (Penguin, 2017) p. 212.

Report of the Climate Change Committee (2021).

Report of the Intergovernmental Panel on Climate Change (2021).

Sayer, Andrew. *Why We Can't Afford The Rich* (Policy Press, 2015).

Scadden, Rosemary. *No Job for a Little Girl: Voices from Domestic Service* (Gomer Press, 2013) p. 51.

Schumacher, E. F. *Small Is Beautiful* (Abacus, 1974).

Skidelski Robert and Skidelski Edward. *How Much Is Enough? Money and the Good Life* (Penguin, 2013).

REFERENCES

Titmuss, Richard. *Poverty and Population* (Macmillan, 1938).

Wales: The Way Ahead (Cardiff, HMSO, 1967).

Webb, Harri. *Looking Up England's Arsehole*, ed. Meic Stephens (Y Lolfa, 2000) pp. 10–11.

Williams, Chris. *Democratic Rhondda* (University of Wales Press, 1996).

Williams, Gwyn A. *When Was Wales?* (Penguin Books, 1985).

Williams, L. and Boyns, T. *Occupation in Wales,1831–1971* (Bulletin of Economic Research, Vol. 29, 1977).

Wilkinson and Pickett. *The Spirit Level: Why Equality is Better for Everyone* (Penguin, 2010).

Modern Wales by Parthian Books

The Modern Wales Series, edited by Dai Smith and supported by the Rhys Davies Trust, was launched in 2017. The Series offers an extensive list of biography, memoir, history and politics which reflect and analyse the development of Wales as a modernised society into contemporary times. It engages widely across places and people, encompasses imagery and the construction of iconography, dissects historiography and recounts plain stories, all in order to elucidate the kaleidoscopic pattern which has shaped and changed the complex culture and society of Wales and the Welsh.

The inaugural titles in the Series were *To Hear the Skylark's Song*, a haunting memoir of growing up in Aberfan by Huw Lewis, and Joe England's panoramic *Merthyr: The Crucible of Modern Wales*. The impressive list has continued with Angela John's *Rocking the Boat*, essays on Welsh women who pioneered the universal fight for equality and Daryl Leeworthy's landmark overview *Labour Country*, on the struggle through radical action and social democratic politics to ground Wales in the civics of common ownership. Myths and misapprehension, whether naïve or calculated, have been ruthlessly filleted in Martin Johnes's startling *Wales: England's Colony?* and a clutch of biographical studies will reintroduce us to the once seminal, now neglected, figures of Cyril Lakin, Minnie Pallister and Gwyn Thomas, whilst Meic Stephens's *Rhys Davies: A Writer's Life* and Dai Smith's *Raymond Williams: A Warrior's Tale* form part of an associated back catalogue from Parthian.

the RHYS DAVIES TRUST

WALES: ENGLAND'S COLONY?

Martin Johnes

From the very beginnings of Wales, its people have defined themselves against their large neighbour. This book tells the fascinating story of an uneasy and unequal relationship between two nations living side-by-side.

PB / £8.99
978-1-912681-41-9

RHYS DAVIES: A WRITER'S LIFE

Meic Stephens

Rhys Davies (1901-78) was among the most dedicated, prolific and accomplished of Welsh prose writers. This is his first full biography.

'This is a delightful book, which is itself a social history in its own right, and funny.'
– The Spectator

PB / £11.99
978-1-912109-96-8

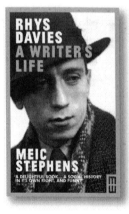

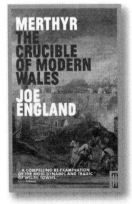

MERTHYR, THE CRUCIBLE OF MODERN WALES

Joe England

Merthyr Tydfil was the town where the future of a country was forged: a thriving, struggling surge of people, industry, democracy and ideas. This book assesses an epic history of Merthyr from 1760 to 1912 through the focus of a fresh and thoroughly convincing perspective.

PB / £18.99
978-1-913640-05-7

TO HEAR THE SKYLARK'S SONG

Huw Lewis

To Hear the Skylark's Song is a memoir about how Aberfan survived and eventually thrived after the terrible disaster of the 21st of October 1966.

'A thoughtful and passionate memoir, moving and respectful.'
– Tessa Hadley

PB / £8.99
978-1-912109-72-2

ROCKING THE BOAT

Angela V. John

This insightful and revealing collection of essays focuses on seven Welsh women who, in a range of imaginative ways, resisted the status quo in Wales, England and beyond during the nineteenth and twentieth centuries.

PB / £11.99
978-1-912681-44-0

TURNING THE TIDE

Angela V. John

This rich biography tells the remarkable tale of Margaret Haig Thomas (1883-1958) who became the second Viscountess Rhondda. She was a Welsh suffragette, held important posts during the First World War and survived the sinking of the *Lusitania*.

PB / £17.99
978-1-909844-72-8

BRENDA CHAMBERLAIN, ARTIST & WRITER

Jill Piercy

The first full-length biography of Brenda Chamberlain chronicles the life of an artist and writer whose work was strongly affected by the places she lived, most famously Bardsey Island and the Greek island of Hydra.

PB / £11.99
978-1-912681-06-8

PARTHIAN

MODERN WALES

RAYMOND WILLIAMS: A WARRIOR'S TALE

Dai Smith

Raymond Williams (1921-1998) was the most influential socialist writer and thinker in post-war Britain. Now, for the first time, making use of Williams's private and unpublished papers and by placing him in a wide social and cultural landscape, Dai Smith, in this highly original and much praised biography, uncovers how Williams's life to 1961 is an explanation of his immense intellectual achievement.

'Becomes at once the authoritative account... Smith has done all that we can ask the historian as biographer to do.'
– Stefan Collini, *London Review of Books*

PB / £16.99
978-1-913640-08-8

BETWEEN WORLDS: A QUEER BOY FROM THE VALLEYS

Jeffrey Weeks

A man's own story from the Rhondda. Jeffrey Weeks was born in the Rhondda in 1945, of mining stock. As he grew up he increasingly felt an outsider in the intensely community-minded valleys, a feeling intensified as he became aware of his gayness. Escape came through education. He left for London, to university, and to realise his sexuality. He has been described as the 'most significant British intellectual working on sexuality to emerge from the radical sexual movements of the 1970s'.

HB / £20
978-1-912681-88-4